Rails 5 Revealed

Alan Bradburne

Apress®

Rails 5 Revealed

Alan Bradburne
Reading, United Kingdom

ISBN-13 (pbk): 978-1-4842-1708-5   ISBN-13 (electronic): 978-1-4842-1709-2
DOI 10.1007/978-1-4842-1709-2

Managing Director: Welmoed Spahr
Lead Editor: Steve Anglin
Technical Reviewer: Eldon Alameda
Editorial Board: Steve Anglin, Pramila Balan, Louise Corrigan, Jonathan Gennick, Robert
    Hutchinson, Celestin Suresh John, Michelle Lowman, James Markham, Susan McDermott,
    Matthew Moodie, Douglas Pundick, Ben Renow-Clarke, Gwenan Spearing
Coordinating Editor: Mark Powers
Compositor: SPi Global
Indexer: SPi Global
Artist: SPi Global

Distributed to the book trade worldwide by Springer Science+Business Media New York, 233 Spring Street, 6th Floor, New York, NY 10013. Phone 1-800-SPRINGER, fax (201) 348-4505, e-mail orders-ny@springer-sbm.com, or visit www.springeronline.com. Apress Media, LLC is a California LLC and the sole member (owner) is Springer Science + Business Media Finance Inc (SSBM Finance Inc). SSBM Finance Inc is a **Delaware** corporation.

For information on translations, please e-mail rights@apress.com, or visit www.apress.com.

Apress and friends of ED books may be purchased in bulk for academic, corporate, or promotional use. eBook versions and licenses are also available for most titles. For more information, reference our Special Bulk Sales–eBook Licensing web page at www.apress.com/bulk-sales.

Any source code or other supplementary materials referenced by the author in this text are available to readers at www.apress.com/9781484217085. For detailed information about how to locate your book's source code, go to www.apress.com/source-code/. Readers can also access source code at SpringerLink in the Supplementary Material section for each chapter.

Printed on acid-free paper

For Rion

Contents at a Glance

Contents

About the Author

Alan Bradburne is a software developer specializing in Ruby on Rails.

Alan has been programming computers since receiving a ZX81 at the age of eight. He has been developing web applications since 1997 and working with Rails since 2004.

Since 2002, Alan has provided freelance development, training, and consulting services to companies worldwide, ranging from startups to multinationals. Along the way, he's co-founded a number of startups, launched numerous sites and apps, and has had the privilege of speaking at conferences worldwide.

Alan lives in Reading, UK, (with frequent spells in Kumamoto, Japan) with his wife, Mayumi, and son, Rion. You can find him online at http://alanbradburne.com and @alanb on Twitter.

About the Technical Reviewer

Eldon Alameda is a web developer who currently resides in the harsh climates of Kansas. He works as a regional webmaster for the US National Weather Service. Prior to this, he did development for a variety of companies, including local startups, advertising firms, Sprint PCS, and IBM. During the 1990s, he also acquired a nice stack of worthless stock options from working for dot-com companies.

Acknowledgments

This book wouldn't exist without the assistance and support of many people.

First of all, I would like to thank Mark Powers from Apress for his support, patience, perseverance, and assistance in helping me write this book. Also, many thanks to all the people behind the scenes at Apress that have helped produce this book.

Thank you, Eldon Alameda for doing a fantastic job in reviewing and helping me clarify my writing. Knowing that such an experienced developer is reviewing the book helped my confidence greatly.

I want to say a huge thank you to every single committer to Rails for their seemingly tireless work in constantly improving this incredible framework. It's amazing to see how strong the momentum still is to make Rails the best it can be.

When David Heinemeier Hansson unleashed the very first release of Rails back in 2004, it was a hugely pivotal moment for me, rejuvenating my love of web development, and subsequently opening up so many opportunities. Thank you, David.

My parents kick-started my interest in computers and supported and encouraged me ever since. Thank you, Mum and Dad, for believing in me.

I couldn't have written this book without the incredible support and encouragement of my wife, Mayumi. I'm so happy to be sharing my life with you. Thank you for everything.

My son, Rion, brightens every day and gives me so much hope for the future. I treasure every single moment and watching you grow and learn is the most wonderful gift ever.

Introduction

When Rails was first conceived, the web and the web development industry was a very different place. The concept of Internet-connected mobile devices was still in its infancy, dynamically updating pages were almost unheard of, and development was often bogged down by overly complex frameworks or expensive licensing fees. Rails turned this world upside down and helped to kick-start a renaissance in web development. But Rails has never stool still, and with each release, the developers have constantly pushed to make elegant yet flexible solutions to complex problems.

Rails 5 is an evolution of Rails 4.2, but with the addition of Action Cable and the inclusion of Rails API, it brings it right up to date with modern web development practices. Rails has always excelled at allowing solo developers and small teams to tackle huge projects and complex problems, and this exemplified by the thought and work behind these features.

This book aims to get you up to speed as quickly as possible with the new features of Rails 5. Action Cable is an especially exciting addition to the Rails toolbox and the elegance and simplicity with which you can add real-time features to your site should not be understated. It will be very exciting to see how developers make use of it.

I'm really excited by the release of Rails 5 and, in writing this book, I have had a chance to explore many of these features in depth. I hope that a taste of the new features also gets you excited about the possibilities. And I hope you find the book useful and informative.

Since this book was finished before the final release of Rails 5, while I have endeavored to incorporate as many late-breaking details, there may be some small changes or last-minute additions to the release that didn't make it into the book. I will attempt to note these on the book's errata page on Apress.com and on my personal site, `http://alanbradburne.com`

I welcome all constructive feedback. You can contact me at `alan@alanbradburne.com` and @alanb on Twitter. I look forward to hearing from you!

CHAPTER 1

Upgrading to Rails 5

This chapter covers the process of upgrading an existing Rails 4.2 application to Rails 5. While I obviously cannot cover every situation and mixture of gems and configurations, I describe the general upgrade procedure and point out the required changes to your application.

Moving a complex existing application to a major new version of Rails can be stressful, but with good test coverage and a methodical approach, it should be a straightforward process.

Test Coverage

Before you begin the upgrade process, you should take a look at your application's test coverage. Having a solid suite of tests for your application, including end-to-end integration tests, is an important way to help you ensure that the upgrade to a new version of Rails hasn't broken any existing functionality.

If you find there are areas of your application that are lacking in test coverage, please consider spending some time addressing this before you start moving your application to Rails 5.

Once you are happy with the state of your test suite, then it's time to continue.

Upgrading Ruby

Before you touch your Rails application, you must ensure that the version of Ruby you are using is 2.2.2 or above. At the time of writing, the latest version of Ruby is 2.3.0. Since Ruby 2.3 features a number of performance and memory management improvements, you should use it, if possible.

How you upgrade your Ruby installation depends entirely on the setup of your development environment on your local machine.

Electronic supplementary material The online version of this chapter (doi:10.1007/978-1-4842-1709-2_1) contains supplementary material, which is available to authorized users.

If you are using OS X or Linux, then you are likely to be using rbenv, RVM, or chruby, so upgrading should be a simple matter of building and switching to the necessary version.

If you are running Windows, rubyinstaller.org has installers available for up-to-date versions of Ruby.

Of course, if you intend to upgrade any production applications to Rails 5, you must ensure that your production servers are upgraded to a suitable version of Rails before you deploy your application. Depending on the version of Rails that your application is currently using, it may not be compatible with Ruby 2.3.0, so you must take that into account when upgrading and planning your deployment.

You should specify the Ruby version in your application's Gemfile. Do this by placing the ruby directive in your Gemfile. For example:

```
ruby '2.3.0'
```

While this is not a requirement, it is good practice because it ensures that all the developers working on your project and your test and deployed versions are running on the same release of Ruby.

Upgrading the Rails Gem

Once you're happy with your application's test coverage and you have ensured that you have the up-to-date version of Ruby, it's time to switch your application to Rails 5.

Before you move to Rails 5, you should ensure that your application works fine on the most recent version of Rails 4.2 (at the time of writing, it is version 4.2.5.1) in order to ensure that you spot any deprecation warnings or have other issues with your application that aren't a result of the move to Rails 5.

Now change the specified version of Rails in your Gemfile to 5.0.0:

```
gem 'rails', '5.0.0'
```

Then run the bundle update command, specifying to update the Rails gem.

```
$ bundle update rails
```

This installs the latest Rails gem, along with all the necessary dependencies. If you look at the differences in your Gemfile.lock before and after the bundle update, you see that all of the Rails-related gems (such as activerecord, actionpack, and actionview) have been upgraded. You also notice a new addition, actioncable.

The rack gem has been updated to the latest version of the Rack 2 gem. Rails 5 is not compatible with older versions of Rack.

Rails Update

You should now run the Rails update command to update the Rails support files, such as the default configuration files and initializers.

To initiate this, enter the following command:

```
$ rails rails:update
```

This command checks all the relevant files; it skips identical ones, creates new files, and asks for permission to update any conflicting ones.

You should be very careful and examine each file when a conflict prompt is shown. For example:

```
conflict  config/environments/production.rb
Overwrite /Users/alan/Projects/Sensors/config/environments/production.rb?
(enter "h" for help) [Ynaqdh]
```

Pressing the D key shows the difference between the current version and the version that would replace it. Either use this to update your local file manually, or overwrite your file and then add your edits.

Be sure to take a look at all the files there were added or changed by this process to understand if there are any implications for your application.

ApplicationRecord As the Base Class for ActiveRecord Models

By default in Rails 5, when you generate a new model, it is created to inherit from a model called ApplicationRecord.

This is similar to how Rails controllers inherit from ApplicationController. It gives you a place to keep common methods and behaviors for your models.

The model generator checks in your app/models directory; if a file application_record.rb exists, it uses that as the superclass for the model being generated, rather than ActiveRecord::Base.

Since this is the preferred new behavior for Rails 5, you should create the app/models/application_record.rb file and enter the class, as shown in Listing 1-1.

Listing 1-1. The New Default ApplicationRecord Base Class

```
class ApplicationRecord < ActiveRecord::Base
  self.abstract_class = true
end
```

You should then update your existing model files to inherit from this. For example, change

```
class Product < ActiveRecord::Base
```

to

```
class Product < ApplicationRecord
```

While doing this isn't mandatory, it is the expected and preferred behavior for Rails 5 applications, so it makes sense to bring your application up to date.

3

ApplicationJob As the Base Class for ActiveJob Jobs

Similar to `ActiveModel` classes now having the `ApplicationRecord` superclass, newly generated `ActiveJob` jobs inherits from `ApplicationJob` if the `app/jobs/application_job.rb` file exists.

To keep in line with this behavior, you should create the `app/jobs/application_job.rb` file with the class definition in Listing 1-2.

Listing 1-2. The New Default ApplicationJob Base Class

```
class ApplicationJob < ActiveJob::Base
end
```

Then update any existing job classes to inherit from this by changing the superclass. For example, change

```
class CalculateRatingsJob < ActiveJob::Base
```

to

```
class CalculateRatingsJob < ApplicationJob
```

While the default `ApplicationJob` class is empty, you should look at moving any methods or configurations shared by all of your jobs to the superclass.

Upgrade to PostgreSQL 9.1 or Later

If you are using PostgreSQL as the database for your application, you must ensure that you are using PostgreSQL version 9.1 or higher. Previous versions are past their end-of-life date and support for them has been dropped from Rails 5.

Devise Gem

If your application makes use of the popular Devise gem for authentication, you need to change your Gemfile to use the most up-to-date commit from Devise's page on the GitHub repository. At the time of writing, there is no official versioned release of Devise that is compatible with Rails 5; but the required changes have been committed to GitHub.

To do this, edit your Gemfile and change the entry for Devise as follows:

```
gem 'devise', git: 'git@github.com:plataformatec/devise.git'
```

You must then perform this:

```
$ bundle update devise
```

If you attempt to use an older version of Devise, you encounter the following error:

```
uninitialized constant ActionController::RackDelegation
```

Devise is a very popular gem, so this is a common problem to encounter when updating an app to Rails 5.

Callback Chain Changes

Rails 5 has slightly changed the behavior of callback chains.

In Rails 5, the preferred method to halt a callback chain is to explicitly call throw(:abort); whereas in previous versions of Rails, you could simply return false from a callback method.

When you upgrade an old application to Rails 5, the application still performs as expected, but you receive deprecation warnings. Once you have brought your application up to date, you can fully enable the new behavior and remove the deprecation warnings by adding an initializer file containing this line:

```
ActiveSupport.halt_callback_chains_on_return_false = false
```

New applications created with the Rails 5 application generator already include this config statement.

This change is discussed in more detail in Chapter 2.

Running Tests

You should now be ready to run your test suite and start to pick off any necessary gems that require updating, one by one.

Remember, with Rails 5, you run your tests with the rails command rather than rake:

```
$ rails test
```

You will almost certainly find some deprecation warnings and some incompatible gems. Check the support pages for the gems as most will have been updated to work with Rails 5.

Chapter 2 details most of the changes and additions to the Rails API to help you understand how to update your application.

CHAPTER 2

Changes from Rails 4.2

In this chapter, I go through the majority of the important changes to Rails, excluding Active Record and the testing framework.

While most of the changes seem small, there are some great refinements of the framework, making your day-to-day development work easier, allowing greater configuration and flexibility, and bringing the framework up to date.

I've omitted changes that are simply bug fixes or internal changes that don't affect application development.

Ruby 2.2 or Higher

If you are upgrading from an earlier version of Rails, or just about to start a new Rails 5 project, the very first thing you need to know is that Rails 5 requires Ruby version 2.2.2 or above.

To check your version of Ruby, just use `ruby -v`.

```
$ ruby -v
```

```
ruby 2.2.2p95 (2015-04-13 revision 50295) [x86_64-darwin15]
```

One of the main reasons for requiring Ruby 2.2 is so that Rails can take advantage of the improvements to the garbage collection. In 2.2 and above, symbols are now garbage collected, resulting in improvements in memory management and lower memory usage. Garbage collecting symbols also prevent denial-of-service attacks that could make your application consume ever-increasing amounts of memory.

Ruby 2.2 also uses an improved system called *incremental garbage collection,* resulting in a large performance increase.

If you're interested in learning more about the garbage collector changes, read the blog article by Koichi Sasada at https://engineering.heroku.com/blogs/2015-02-04-incremental-gc/. You can watch his RubyConf presentation about the new GC at http://confreaks.tv/videos/rubyconf2014-incremental-gc-for-ruby-interpreter.

Also, Rails 5 makes extensive use of keyword arguments to tidy up a lot of code. The keyword arguments feature was introduced in Ruby 2.1.

© Alan Bradburne 2016
A. Bradburne, *Rails 5 Revealed,* DOI 10.1007/978-1-4842-1709-2_2

To take advantage of the new Ruby features, the improved garbage collector, and the speed and security enhancements, the core team decided to drop support for older versions of Ruby.

Ruby 2.3.0 was released in December 2015, and at the time of writing, it is the recommend version of Ruby because it contains a number of performance enhancements.

Rails Commands

In this section, I go through changes to Rails commands.

Rake Tasks

Another change that you'll quickly come across is the multitude of rake tasks that you use in day-to-day Rails development—such as db:migrate, assets:precompile, and test—have all been aggregated under the rails command.

So, for instance,

```
$ rake db:migrate
```

simply becomes

```
$ rails db:migrate
```

The thinking behind this is that it's confusing to have a separation between the two— using rake for some things and rails for other tasks. Using rails for everything means you never have to worry about which to use.

To get full details of all available tasks, use the following:

```
$ rails --help
```

Rails Restart

A new command has been added to the application admin tasks: rails restart. This command is simply a convenience method that touches the tmp/restart.txt file within your application, indicating to Spring (the process that starts and controls the Rails development process) that the application should be restarted.

```
$ rails restart
```

Rails Initializers

The rails initializers command is newly added. It lists the complete set of initializers that are run (and the order that they are run in) when your application is started.

```
$ rails initializers
```

```
set_load_path

...

eager_load!

finisher_hook

set_routes_reloader_hook

set_clear_dependencies_hook

disable_dependency_loading
```

The update Command

A new script has been added to the bin directory of a generated application: update. You can use this script to automatically update your development environment, which is useful after you have pulled someone else's changes from your source control.

The script performs the following tasks:

- Ensures that the bundler gem is installed
- Runs bundle install
- Performs any database migrations with db:migrate
- Clears your application's log files and tmp directory
- Restarts your application

```
$ bin/update
```

```
== Installing dependencies ==

The Gemfile's dependencies are satisfied

== Updating database ==

== Removing old logs and tempfiles ==

== Restarting application server ==
```

Development Cache Toggle

A small addition to the available rake commands is the ability to quickly enable and disable the cache for development mode. Obviously, this was possible before, but it required editing the config file and restarting the server. Having it available as a rails command just makes it more convenient.

```
$ rails dev:cache
```

```
Development mode is now being cached.
```

This can quickly be turned off again by repeating the following command:

```
$ rails dev:cache
```

```
Development mode is no longer being cached.
```

You can also start your development server with caching enabled or disabled, which overrides the settings in the environment file by using the options --dev-caching or --no-dev-caching.

```
$ rails server --dev-caching
```

Beyond Ludicrous Speed

The Rails 5 release includes a pull request by Richard Schneeman that has the tantalizing title "Beyond Ludicrous Speed." This PR is the result of extensive investigation and benchmarking work by Schneeman to make a number of seemingly minor changes to the Rails internals, such as removing duplicated hashes, freezing strings, and tidying arrays. By doing this, he has dramatically reduced the number of allocated objects, and hence memory used per request, leading to a speed increase of 11.9%.

I highly recommend taking at a look at the pull request at https://github.com/rails/rails/pull/21057 to understand the changes and to see how small changes can have large effects when optimizing your code.

The best part of this feature is that it requires no change on your part; nothing has changed externally—you can just enjoy the performance increase!

Asset Serving

You are likely aware that Rails has a built-in server for serving public assets such as JavaScript, CSS, and image files.

In most applications, you'll likely use the static asset server in development and test mode, but make use of your web server's assets serving in production mode. However, if you host a Rails application on Heroku, your assets are served directly by Rails.

As part of the Rails 5 upgrade, the built-in asset server had an overhaul. Previously, you had very little control over how static assets were served. Apart from enabling and disabling the server, the only setting you could change was the cache-control header. This means that you are unable to set additional headers, such as Expires.

Public File Server

The previous config settings—static_cache_control and server_static_files—have been deprecated as of Rails 5; they will be completely removed in Rails 5.1.

In their place is the new public_file_server configuration. The two settings are now set by the enabled and headers attributes of the public_file_server config setting, where the headers attribute allows you to set any headers, not just cache-control.

To update an older application, make the following changes.

```
config.serve_static_files = true
```

becomes

```
config.public_file_server.enabled = true
```

And the cache_control is just one of the file server headers.

```
config.static_cache_control = 'public, max-age=172800'
```

becomes

```
config.public_file_server.headers = {
  'Cache-Control': 'public, max-age=172800'
}
```

The following is an example with the Expires header:

```
config.public_file_server.enabled = true
config.public_file_server.headers = {
  'Cache-Control': 'public, max-age=172800',
  'Expires': "#{1.month.from_now.to_formatted_s(:rfc822)}"
}
```

Obviously, this is settable on a per-environment basis in your config/environments/[environment].rb files; you can set different headers as necessary.

Rendering

This section covers changes to rendering in Rails 5.

Render from Anywhere

Prior to Rails 5, the render method could only be called from within a controller. At first glance, this appears to be a sensible limitation, since it seems to be where you will always need to render views. On occasion, however, you may need to render a template; for instance, from within a background job or a script, or when responding on a web socket.

There have been some gems that provide a work around to this, but Rails 5 allows you to perform a render from anywhere within your application.

To do this, you simply use the render method like this:

```
ApplicationController.render template: 'orders/index.html.erb'
```

You can also call the render method of a specific controller. For example:

```
OrdersController.render :index
```

It's likely that when rendering a view template, you will need to assign objects so that the view can be rendered with the necessary data. When calling render from a controller, you just set variables before calling render, but when calling from outside a controller, you must assign the relevant objects using the assigns option. Also, the usual locals option can be used to pass in local variables. For example:

```
OrdersController.render :show, locals: { user: current_user }, assigns:
{ order: order }
```

The actual renderer object is accessible via the renderer method. You can see the environment that the view template is rendered in by calling the defaults method on this renderer:

```
ApplicationController.renderer.defaults
```

```
=> {:http_host=>"example.org", :https=>false, :method=>"get",
:script_name=>"", :input=>""}
```

By instantiating a new renderer, you can change the environment that the renderer is performed in. For example:

```
orders_renderer = OrdersController.renderer.new(method: 'post', https: true)
```

```
=> #<ActionController::Renderer:0x007fc606a09e10
@controller=OrdersController,
@defaults={:http_host=>"example.org", :https=>false,
:method=>"get", :script_name=>"", :input=>""},
@env={"HTTP_HOST"=>"example.org", "HTTPS"=>"on",
"REQUEST_METHOD"=>"POST", "SCRIPT_NAME"=>"", "rack.input"=>""}>
```

You can subsequently perform render calls on that renderer instance.

Render Nothing Deprecated

The nothing option of the render method has been deprecated; it will be removed in Rails 5.1.

If you wish to respond with no body, simply use the head method instead.

So if you are currently responding to any requests with an empty body, say in an API controller, using this:

```
render nothing: true
```

You need to change it to this:

```
head :ok
```

Of course, you can send any HTTP response, such as :created or :not_found with the head command.

HTTP Cache Forever

Action Controller has gained the http_cache_forever method. It allows you to define an HTTP response that has an expiry date 100 years in the future, meaning that the browser should cache it indefinitely. This is useful for pages that rarely change, such as static pages.

By default, the response is private, meaning that proxies do not cache it, but it is cached on the user's browser. By specifying that the response is public, it is also cached by proxy servers.

The method also allows you to set a version string. By changing this version string, the ETag that is used to check if the cached data requires updating is updated, busting the cache.

Listing 2-1 shows an example controller where the response to the index method will be cached indefinitely on the user's browser and any proxies.

Listing 2-1. Caching a Static Response

```
class StaticController < ApplicationController
  def index
    http_cache_forever(public: true, version: 'v1') do
      render plain: 'hello'
    end
  end
end
```

Multiple Root Routes

It is now possible to set multiple root routes in your routes.rb file. This is useful if you need to specify different routes based on constraints.

For example:

```
root 'blog#show', constraints: ->(req) { Hostname.blog_site?(req.host) }
root 'home#show'
```

If the request meets the conditions set by the constraints block, then the first root is used; otherwise, it falls back to the second one. This was possible in earlier versions of Rails by using a get route; but the change allows you to clarify your intentions and makes it possible to always just use the root_path and root_url helpers and have them respond to different conditions.

Static Index

A new configuration option that allows you to set the file shown as the static index has been added.

By default, Rails looks for a file called index.html in the public directory. If you wish to change this, add the setting to your config/application.rb file, as follows:

```
config.static_index = 'main'
```

Active Model

This section covers changes in the active model.

Halting the Callback Chain

Previously in Rails, when you had a before callback for a model, if that callback method returned false, then the callback chain would be halted, the save method would return false, and save! would raise a RecordNotSaved exception.

In Rails 5, the preferred method to halt a callback chain is to explicitly call `throw(:abort)`.

If the `halt_callback_chains_on_return_false` config setting is set to `true`, then returning `false` still has the desired effect, but you receive a deprecation warning; otherwise, returning `false` does not halt the callback chain, so ensure that you update any existing applications.

XML Serializer Removed

Rails 5 has removed `ActiveModel::Serializers::Xml`, which means that you can no longer perform `to_xml` on an object. It was removed simply because it wasn't used by the majority of Rails applications.

If you still require XML serialization, you can simply install the `activemodel-serializers-xml` gem to restore this functionality.

The Case Sensitive Option for Confirmation Validator

There is now a new option for the confirmation validator: the ability to make the validation case insensitive.

Previously, if you defined a confirmation validation, let's say on an email address, the `email` and `email_confirmation` attributes must be identical, including the case.

By setting `case_sensitve: false`, you can make this validation case insensitive. For example:

```
class User << ActiveRecord::Base
  validates :email, confirmation: { case_sensitive: false }
end

> user = User.new(email: 'alan@kumacode.co.uk', email_confirmation: 'ALAN@
KUMACODE.CO.UK')

> user.valid?
```

```
=> true
```

validates_acceptance_of Accepts True

A small change to the `validates_acceptance_of` validation is that now both 1 and `true` are accepted as acceptance. Previously, the validation accepted only 1 as acceptance and it would be returned from an HTML form. You could add an `accept: true` option if you needed to validate a database column. But now, both values are acceptable, which allows simplification in models using this feature.

Dirty Model Accessor Methods

Two new methods allow you to query the changes to an object after an object has been saved directly for a given attribute.

Previously, once an object was saved, changes were only accessible through the previous_changes method, which listed all changed attributes.

To make the API consistent with how the changes before saving are accessible, you can now query [attribute]_previously_changed? and [attribute]_previous_change.

For example:

```
> user.name = "Alan"
```

```
=> "Alan"
```

```
> user.save
```

```
=> true
```

```
> user.name_previously_changed?
```

```
=> true
```

```
> user.name_previous_change
```

```
=> [nil, "Alan"]
```

Action Mailer

Now let's look at changes in the action mailer.

Force the SSL Setting Used for Mailer URLs

The Rails config.force_ssl = true configuration setting now automatically sets the mailer configuration options to ensure that any URLs generated by the mailer templates use HTTPS as the protocol. This effectively sets the following option for you:

```
config.action_mailer.default_url_options = { protocol: 'https' }`
```

Deliver Later Queue Name

The Active Job queue used to be set to mailers. It is now configurable simply by setting the following config attribute:

```
config.action_mailer.deliver_later_queue_name = "email_queue"
```

16

Templates User Default Locale and Fallbacks

When selecting which mailer template to use, Rails 5 now properly respects the default locale of the application; whereas previously, a template without any locale specified would be used.

Email Template *_path Helpers Deprecated

The *_path helpers have been deprecated in template files. The reason for this is that any links in emails must be an absolute URL, rather than a relative path. Hopefully, *_path helpers were never used in any email templates; but now they've been deprecated to ensure that they aren't!

Remove deliver and deliver! Methods

The deliver and deliver! methods have been removed as of Rails 5. They were deprecated in Rails 4.2, so you should already have switched to using the deliver_later and deliver_now replacements, but it's worth checking to ensure that the old methods aren't still in your application.

Class Naming Follows Rails Conventions

When you generate a new mailer using the Rails generator, they are now created following the Rails convention of using a suffix for the type of class—in this case, _mailer.

```
$ rails g mailer User
```

```
    create    app/mailers/user_mailer.rb

    create    app/mailers/application_mailer.rb

    invoke    erb

    create    app/views/user_mailer

    create    app/views/layouts/mailer.text.erb

    create    app/views/layouts/mailer.html.erb

    invoke    test_unit

    create    test/mailers/user_mailer_test.rb

    create    test/mailers/previews/user_mailer_preview.rb
```

Internationalization

There is one change in internationalization.

Pick up New Locales Without Restart

If you have spent time localizing an application, you know that new locale files are only picked up when the Rails server is restarted.

When running in the development environment in Rails 5, I18n.load_path is automatically reloaded, so you don't need to restart the server to make new locale files available.

Active Job

This section covers changes to Active Job.

ApplicationJob Base Class

In previous versions of Rails, each background job generated simply inherited from ActiveJob::Base. Until you generated a job class, the app/jobs directory didn't exist.

In Rails 5, all generated applications include an app/jobs directory that contains an application_job.rb file. All newly generated job classes inherit from this ApplicationJob class.

This follows the same conventions as controllers and mailers using an Application* class as the base class. It allows you to set up application-wide settings and methods.

If you are upgrading from a previous version of Rails, you should change your jobs to this style.

Keywords in Process Methods

The Active Job perform method now lets you use keyword arguments.

Previously, you were limited to passing only a series of unnamed arguments. If you wanted to use named parameters, you had to pass a hash to the perform_later method. For example:

```
def perform(hash)
  image_id = hash[:image_id]
  processing_options = hash[:options)
  # do image processing
end
```

But Rails 5 allows you to use regular Ruby keyword arguments in your perform_later method call.

For example, a job could be defined as shown in Listing 2-2.

Listing 2-2. Active Job using Keyword Arguments

```
class ImageProcessJob < ApplicationJob
  queue_as :default

  def perform(image_id: image_id, processing_options: options)
    # image_id and processing_options are now available!
    # do image processing
  end
end
```

and called with the following command:

```
ImageProcessJob.perform_later(image_id: image.id, processing_options: "-s 300x300")
```

Defaults to Async Queue Adaptor

Previously, Active Job did not have a default queue adaptor setup. Without defining one, Active Job would not allow you to create new jobs until you had configured it properly.

Rails 5 defaults to the :async queue adaptor, which means that when you start a new application, you can develop using background jobs right away, without worrying about configuration first.

The async adaptor uses a concurrent Ruby thread pool to process the jobs asynchronously outside of the main request, but within the same system process. This means that it doesn't require any external dependencies or configuration. However, it is only suitable for development and test environments; you should never use it in production.

Job Priorities

Active Job allows you to place jobs on different queues, which in turn can have different priority levels. For instance, you may have a clean-up job queue that can run at a very low priority, but a mailer queue that runs on a high priority.

Previously, the priority of these queues had to be set manually when configuring your choice of back end (e.g., Sidekiq, Resque, or Delayed Job).

However, for back ends that support it, Rails 5 allows you to override the priority level of the job in the job class. Listing 2-3 shows an example of this.

Listing 2-3. Active Job Class Using Queue Priority

```
class ImageProcessJob < ApplicationJob
  queue_with_priority 50

  def perform(image_id: image_id, processing_options: options)
    # do image processing
  end
end
```

Note that at the time of writing this is only currently supported by Delayed Job and Que; for other backed Active Jobs, the priority level must be set per queue.

Other Changes

Finally, let's look at some miscellaneous changes.

Mime Type Constants Deprecated

Up until now, when dealing with MIME types within Rails, it was normal to use constants such as `Mime::HTML` or `Mime::JSON`.

As of Rails 5, these constants are deprecated. They are now accessible through accessors like `Mime[:html]` and `Mime[:json]`.

Since using the `Mime[:html]` format is valid in older versions of Rails too, you should consider updating older applications and libraries.

Documentation Generating Tasks Removed

The `doc:app`, `doc:rails`, and `doc:guides` documentation generation tasks have all been removed. This is simply because they were rarely used. Developers appear to prefer to use online documentation.

Removing these tasks from the Rails gem means that they no longer need to be maintained. It also means that the entire Rails documentation doesn't need to be bundled with every download of the Rails gem.

method_source Gem

To aid with debugging, the `method_source` gem has been included as a dependency. This gem allows you to display the source or comments for any method. When used in conjunction with the development console, this can be very useful.

Even though the gem is installed, to use it, you need to require it:

```
> require 'method_source'
```

```
=> true
```

You can then use the `source` and `comment` methods on the `method` method, passing the name of the method that you wish to view.

For example, I can view the source of the `process` method for an instance of my Order class by using `method(:process).source`.

```
> puts Order.first.method(:process).source
```

```
  Order Load (1.0ms)  SELECT  "orders".* FROM "orders" ORDER BY
"orders"."id" ASC LIMIT 1

  def process

    # Do complicated processing here

  end
=> nil
```

By using this, you can also view the source and comments on any Rails method, making it a very useful tool for development and debugging.

```
> puts User.first.orders.method(:load).comment
```

```
  User Load (1.0ms)  SELECT  "users".* FROM "users" ORDER BY "users"."id"
  ASC LIMIT 1
# Causes the records to be loaded from the database if they have not

# been loaded already. You can use this if for some reason you need

# to explicitly load some records before actually using them. The

# return value is the relation itself, not the records.

#

#    Post.where(published: true).load # => #<ActiveRecord::Relation>
=> nil
```

This also works on dynamically generated methods.

▓ **Note**   There are discussions about adding this functionality into future versions of Ruby. If that happens, it's highly likely that the method_source gem will be removed and Rails will rely directly on the Ruby feature.

Autoload All Concerns

Rails 4 added the concept of *concerns*, which provides better support for abstracting reusable code from classes. Previously, Rails only automatically loaded concerns from within the app/controllers/concerns and app/models/concerns directories.

Now, Rails 5 autoloads any concerns from within any subdirectory of app; so if you create `app/mailers/concerns` then any files within there are automatically loaded and available to mailers.

div_for and content_tag_for Helpers Removed

The `div_for` and `content_tag` view helpers have been removed as of Rails 5. If you still require them, you can restore their functionality by simply adding the `record_tag_helper` gem to your application.

CHAPTER 3

Active Record

Active Record is a vital part of the majority of Rails applications, so it's great to see that it is constantly being refined, optimized, and improved upon. The Rails 4.2 release brought large performance improvements and Rails 5 improves upon this further still.

It goes without saying that many hundreds of small bug fixes and tweaks have been committed to the latest version of Active Record, but in this chapter, I concentrate on the biggest and most important changes and additions, and I note any relevant fixes.

The Arel OR Condition

Rails 5 adds a very useful or condition to the Active Record Query Interface, equivalent to using the OR condition in SQL.

Previously, to perform an OR database query, such as

```
SELECT * FROM users WHERE name='Mary' OR height > 179
```

you either had to fall back to using SQL directly or use the underlying Arel table information. For example:

```
t = User.arel_table
results = User.where(t[:name].eq('Mary').or(t[:height].gt(179)))
```

In Rails 5, you can directly use the or query using the following syntax:

```
User.where(name: 'Mary').or(User.where('height > ?', 179))
```

has_secure_token

A small but very useful addition to Rails 5 is has_secure_token. Used in a way similar to the ActiveRecord::Base#has_secure_password method, it specifies that an attribute of your model should be used to store a unique 24-character alphanumeric token.

Tokens such as this are often used in Rails applications for providing token-based API access or allowing one-time access for password reset actions. Since it is such a common use case, it's very convenient to have it built into Rails.

© Alan Bradburne 2016
A. Bradburne, *Rails 5 Revealed*, DOI 10.1007/978-1-4842-1709-2_3

To add a secure token column to an existing model, you can use the migration generator:

```
rails g migration add_auth_token_to_users auth_token:token
```

This creates a migration to add a string column called auth_token and adds a unique index on that column, as shown in Listing 3-1.

Listing 3-1. Migration to Add a Secure Token to a Model

```
class AddAuthTokenToUsers < ActiveRecord::Migration
  def change
    add_column :users, :auth_token, :string
    add_index :users, :auth_token, unique: true
  end
end
```

You then need to add the has_secure_token statement to the relevant model, as shown in Listing 3-2.

Listing 3-2. Class with Secure Token Defined

```
class User < ActiveRecord::Base
  has_secure_token :auth_token
end
```

The name of the model attribute defaults to token if no name for the column is specified.

The actual token value is generated in a before_create handler, so the value is only available after you have successfully created an item. After that, the value does not subsequently change, as shown here:

```
$ user = User.new
$ user.auth_token
```

```
nil
```

```
$ user.save
$ user.auth_token
```

```
=> "MsCqa4Ki3z4okKvH7s3F3FD4"
```

At the time of writing, there is an open issue concerning the fact that some databases (including MySQL) create columns as case insensitive by default. Since the auth token generated by Rails is a case-sensitive base 58 string, it's possible that two different keys would be considered the same, even though they have a different case.

If you are using MySQL, you should read the discussion at `https://github.com/rails/rails/issues/20133`. Make sure that my changing the `auth_token` column type is taken into account.

Multiple Tokens

You can specify multiple token attributes in a model, simply by adding additional `has_secure_token` statements, as shown in Listing 3-3.

Listing 3-3. Class with Multiple Secure Tokens

```
class User < ActiveRecord::Base
  has_secure_token :auth_token
  has_secure_token :password_reset_token
end
```

Regenerating the Token

If you need to regenerate the token (say for instance, the user wishes to reset the API key), then you can use `regenerate_*`, specifying the attribute name.

For example, in our earlier examples with the token attribute called `auth_token`, you would use `regenerate_auth_token`.

This regenerates a new token and saves the new value in the database. For example:

```
$ user.auth_token
```

```
=> "MsCqa4Ki3z4okKvH7s3F3FD4"
```

```
$ user.regenerate_token
```

```
=> "LuSLZLvyEn6YjZuwBAhmfdZj"
```

Token Generator Helper

Let's say that you are using the Rails generator to create a new model and to specify the model attributes as part of the helper. For example:

```
rails g model user auth_token:token
```

Along with creating the relevant database migration, the model generator also automatically adds the has_secure_token :auth_token statement to your new model.

Deprecation of Relation#uniq

Rails 4.2 changed the uniq to distinct Active Record query method. The main reason for this was that uniq could be confused with the Array#uniq method; but distinct more closely matches the underlying SQL, which reduces confusion.

The old uniq method was kept as an alias in Rails 4.2 but deprecated as of Rails 5. Simply use distinct instead.

Required belongs_to Value

Prior to Rails 5, belongs_to values for models were optional. For instance, if I have an Orders model that specifies the relationship belongs_to :user, it would be possible for me to create an Order record with a nil user_id by simply not passing a value, or by setting it to nil. Although this is possible, this is rarely the desired behavior; it is quite likely an error.

Let's clarify how it is normally used and how to make it explicit if a nil is acceptable. In Rails 5, attempting to create a record with no associated record (i.e., having a nil value for the belongs_to attribute) results in a validation error.

However, if you wish for nil to be a perfectly valid value for your belongs_to attribute, you can specify that it is an optional value. To do this, simply add the optional keyword, as shown in Listing 3-4.

Listing 3-4. Optional belongs_to in a Rails Model

```
class Order < ActiveRecord::Base
  belongs_to :user, optional: true
end
```

For new applications created using Rails 5, this will be the default behavior. However, if you are upgrading an older application to Rails 5, this feature will be turned off by default, so as not to break existing applications.

If you wish to enable this feature in an application that was created before Rails 5, add the following setting to your config/application.rb file within the config block:

```
config.active_record.belongs_to_required_by_default = true
```

MySQL JSON Data Type

Version 5.7.8 of MySQL introduced support for a native JSON data type. While Active Record support for native JSON columns has existed for a while because it is a feature of PostgreSQL, this support is now extended to MySQL.

To create a new JSON column, simply specify the column type as json in your migration, as shown in Listing 3-5.

Listing 3-5. Migration for a User with a Native JSON Column

```
class CreateUsers < ActiveRecord::Migration
  def change
    create_table :user do |t|
      t.json :settings
    end
  end
end
```

Let's take a quick look at how to store and access data in a native JSON column. Let's say that you have a User model created, as in the preceding example, with the settings column set to have a JSON data type.

To set values within the settings attribute, you can set it at create-time, directly using a hash. For example:

```
user.settings = { colours: ["red", "green"], alerts: true }
```

Or you can set it by using the key string as the accessor:

```
user.settings["colurs"] = ["red", "green]
user.settings["alerts] = true
```

Obviously, setting values by specifying a hash overwrites any existing values unless you merge the new values with the existing ones.

To retrieve values, Rails returns the values of the JSON column as a hash. So for the previous example:

```
user.settings
```

```
=> {"colours"=>["red", "green"], "alerts"=>true}
```

```
user.settings["colours"]
```

```
=> ["red", "green"]
```

Performing a database query based on the values of the JSON data differs from the PostgreSQL JSON implementation, so be aware that this feature is not completely compatible at the database level.

For instance, when using PostgreSQL, you can search within a JSON column called settings with

```
User.where("users.settings->>'alerts' = ?", "true")
```

whereas with MySQL you would use

```
User.where('JSON_EXTRACT(users.settings, "$.alerts") = true')
```

However, since querying based on the contents of a JSON column is not generally a great idea, hopefully, this isn't something that you'll have to deal with often. Adding indexes to JSON columns is possible, but it's definitely simpler and a better practice to use separate fields for those attributes that you need to search on.

▨ **Note**   Notice here that there are inconsistencies with how PostgreSQL and MySQL deal with Boolean values when searching within JSON data.

Enum Prefix and Suffix Definitions

Enums are a great feature of Active Record that allow you to represent a fixed set of attribute values for a given column as an integer in a database field. These values are then dynamically converted to and from the integer for both queries and results.

However, previously, it wasn't possible to have the same enum values for different columns within the same model.

For instance, if you had a Post model with two columns, status and comments_status, it would be impossible to use the same enum values, active and archived for both of them, because there would be a clash for the enum model instance methods, such as visible? and invisible?, as demonstrated here:

```
class Post < ActiveRecord::Base
  enum status: [:active, :archived]
  enum comments_status: [:active, :archived]
end

> post = Post.new
```

```
ArgumentError: You tried to define an enum named "comments_status" on the
model "Post", but this will generate a instance method "active?", which is
already defined by another enum.
```

Rails 5 solves this problem by adding :_prefix and :_suffix options to the enum definition. These options can take either a Boolean value or a symbol.

If the Boolean true is used, the name of the enum is used as the prefix or suffice. If a symbol is used, that value is used as the prefix or suffix.

For the preceding example, you could now define the enums as shown in Listing 3-6.

Listing 3-6. Post Model with Enums

```
class Post < ActiveRecord::Base
  enum status: [:active, :archived], _suffix: true
  enum comments_status: [:active, :archived], _prefix: :comments
end
```

This now allows you to access the status and comments_status separately. Since the status enum specifies the _suffix as true, that means that the active!, archived!, active?, and archived? methods are suffixed with the name of the attribute; that is, status. The following demonstrates this:

```
> post.status
```

```
=> "active"
```

```
> post.archived_status!
> post.active_status?
```

```
=> false
```

Since the comments_status attribute is defined as using the prefix comments, the ! and ? methods are referenced as comments_active and comments_archived, as shown here:

```
> post.comments_active!
> post.comments_status
```

```
=> "active"
```

```
> post.comments_archived?
```

```
=> false
```

Since you can set both _prefix and _suffix, you can create interesting enum definitions, such as:

```
enum font_size: [:small,:large], enum_prefix: :with, enum_suffix: true
```

This allows you to use instance methods such as this:

```
@book.with_small_font_size?
```

UUID Primary Keys

Rails 4 introduced native support for UUID primary keys when using PostgreSQL. However, even after enabling it, each time you create a new database table using the model generator, you must manually go in to edit each migration to set the id type to UUID.

Rails 5 introduces a new generator config option, primary_key_type. By setting this to uuid, all newly generated migrations use a UUID as the primary key.

To make use of this, add the following configuration to your config/application.rb file within the config block, as shown in Listing 3-7.

Listing 3-7. Setting the Generator to Use UUIDs As Primary Keys

```
config.generators do |g|
  g.orm :active_record, primary_key_type: :uuid
end
```

You also need to ensure that the uuid-ossp PostgreSQL extension is enabled. If you haven't already done this, you can use the enable_extension helper method. Create a migration and enable the PostgreSQL extension, as shown in Listing 3-8.

Listing 3-8. Enabling UUID Primary Keys for PostgreSQL

```
class EnableUuidExtension < ActiveRecord::Migration
  def change
    enable_extension 'uuid-ossp'
  end
end
```

From here, creating a new model migration using the Rails generator results in migrations looking as shown in Listing 3-9.

Listing 3-9. Example Migration Using the UUID Primary Key

```
class CreateEvents < ActiveRecord::Migration
  def change
    create_table :events, id: :uuid do |t|
      t.timestamps
    end
  end
end
```

▓ **Note**   Remember that for now, this is a PostgreSQL-only feature.

Left Outer Joins

A new method called `left_outer_joins` (and an alias `left_joins`) has been added to the Active Record query interface, allowing you to use SQL left outer joins. Previously, in order to perform outer joins, you had to use `joins` and raw SQL.

The current `joins` finder method should be used only for inner joins or for creating custom join queries; but any query requiring a left outer join should use the new method.

A query previously written as

```
User.joins("LEFT OUTER JOIN orders ON orders.user_id = users.id")
```

can now be written much more succinctly as this:

```
User.left_outer_joins(:orders)
```

A common use case for left outer joins is when you wish to return a set of records, including those that do not have any related records in the join table.

For example, if you had a Users table in which each user could have many orders, to select all users together with a count of the total number of orders for each user, you could do this:

```
User.left_joins(:orders).select("users.*, COUNT(orders.id)
AS orders_count").group('users.id')
```

Users with no orders would still be present in the results, with an `orders_count` values of 0. If you used the same query but with `joins(:orders)`, any users with 0 orders would be missing from the returned results.

find_by Raises Exception

Not a big change, but one that should solve a few head-scratching moments! The `find_by` and `find_by!` class methods now correctly raise an `ArgumentError` if they are called without any arguments. Before, they would complain with `NoMethodError: undefined method take!`, causing some confusion.

Drop Table if_exists in Migrations

A useful addition to the migration `drop_table` statement is the `if_exists` option.

When dropping an existing table in a migration, if the table has already been removed, then the migration will fail. By adding the `if_exists` keyword, the table drop will only be attempted if the table actually exists.

So for example, to drop the `orders` table in your migration, you would use this:

```
drop_table :orders, if_exists: true
```

Validation Error Details

Rails 5 introduces a new option for returning the details of validation failures.

As you know, if an object fails validation, the reasons the object is invalid are accessible via the errors method. Before Rails 5, this could be serialized with just to_hash or full_messages. These methods return the validation errors with the default error strings, custom messages defined in the validators, or localized strings based on the locale that is set. For instance:

```
user.errors.to_hash
```

```
{:email=>["can't be blank", "is too short (minimum is 5 characters)"]}
```

Rails 5 introduces a new details error serializer that returns the validation errors by returning a symbol representing the error, along with any additional details. The natural-language version of an error messages is not returned.

For example, given the following model:

```
class User < ActiveRecord::Base
  validates :email, presence: true, length: { in: 5..255 }
end
```

An object with an invalid email attribute would return the following error details:

```
> user.valid?
```

```
false
```

```
> user.errors.details
```

```
{:email=>[{:error=>:blank}, {:error=>:too_short, :count=>5}]}
```

This response is perfect for use in an API where you need to return validation failure information to the API client application but the client manages the localization of the error messages itself.

░ **Note** This behavior has also been backported for earlier versions of Rails and can be utilized by including the active_model-errors_details gem.

Support Bidirectional Destroys

In the previous versions of Rails, if you have two models related through a
has_many/belongs_to relationship, you cannot add dependent: :destroy to both
of the relationships statements. Attempting to delete either of these records results
in a circular dependency, with each record attempting to delete the other one, ending in
a Stack Too Deep error.

Rails 5 has addressed this issue and it is now possible to have models, as shown in
Listing 3-10.

Listing 3-10. Models with Bidirection Destroy Dependencies

```
class Entry < ActiveRecord::Base
  has_one :position, dependent: :destroy
end
class Position < ActiveRecord::Base
  belongs_to :entry, dependent: :destroy
end
```

Now, if you have an Entry record that has a related Position record, deleting either of
the records will result in the deletion of the related record.

Summary

As you can see, Rails 5 brings some great improvements to Active Record, including some
very convenient features, such as has_secure_token and making query writing easier and
less error-prone by improving the query interface.

Since the majority of these are new features or features that result in changes to
existing behavior (such as making the belongs_to value mandatory) are disabled by
default when upgrading from a previous version of Rails, you shouldn't encounter many
problems. Of course, having good test coverage is important.

CHAPTER 4

Testing

Since the first version of Rails, testing has been a fully integrated part of the framework. Over the years, the underlying libraries have been improved and the growing experience of Rails developers has meant that the recommended style of testing has been refined.

When Rails was first released, it made use of the Ruby Test::Unit library that was part of the standard Ruby libraries. Over time, many Rails developers moved to a new Behavior Driven Development test framework, RSpec. However, with the release of version 4, Rails moved to MiniTest, a very fast and lightweight testing library. Many Rails developers have since switched from RSpec to MiniTest.

Although a significant number of Rails developers prefer to use RSpec, MiniTest is the default testing framework (and the one that is used to test Rails itself). MiniTest is part of the Ruby standard libraries. It is very simple to understand and has a comprehensive set of features. Even if you're used to using RSpec, it's worth looking at MiniTest.

Rails 5 has received some nice improvements to the official test framework. The overall performance of test running has been improved in Rails 5, partly due to the speed increases across Rails and the move to Ruby 2.2, but also due to the performance investigations of the test stack and improvements made by Aaron Patterson and other Rails contributors.

In this chapter, we look at the changes to the testing framework that you need to be aware of, plus a few nice improvements.

Test Runner

Rails 5 sports an all-new test runner through the improved `rails test` command.

As mentioned earlier in the book, a number of tasks that were previously performed through the rake command have moved to `rails`. The test runner is one of them.

In earlier versions of rails, the entire test suite was run using `rake test`, or just `rake` on its own. Now, the entire test suite is run with the following command:

```
$ rails test
```

The test runner includes a number of very useful features and changes from the way test runs happened in earlier Rails versions.

© Alan Bradburne 2016
A. Bradburne, *Rails 5 Revealed*, DOI 10.1007/978-1-4842-1709-2_4

As with other Rails commands, use the –h or --help option to get the full list of available options:

```
$ rails test --help
```

Defer Failure Output

If you run a test suite with failing tests, the first change that you'll notice is that test failures are displayed as they happen, rather than being deferred to the end of the test run. If you prefer the old-style behavior, you can use the -d or --defer-output option.

For any failing tests, along with details of the failure, now a command is shown on how to run this failing test in isolation. For example:

```
# Running:

...F

Expected: 200

  Actual: 201

rails test test/controllers/todos_controller_test.rb:13
```

You'll immediately notice that the failing test's output display is now simpler and clearer, making it much easier to quickly understand how your test is failing.

Run Tests by Directory, File, or Line

The ability to run single tests in isolation directly from the command line is a very welcome improvement. It was possible in earlier versions, but it was not obvious and it required a number of command-line options.

Look at the following command:

```
rails test test/controllers/todos_controller_test.rb:13
```

It's clear that it runs the test at line 13 of the test/controllers/todos_controller_test.rb file. A copy and paste of that line is far simpler and faster now than it was previously.

In addition to being able to run a single test, you can also run all the tests in a file, such as this:

```
rails test test/controllers/todos_controller_test.rb
```

You can also run all of the tests within a directory. For example:

```
rails test test/controllers
```

Verbose Mode

While not specifically a feature of the test runner (the functionality comes from the MiniTest library itself), another useful feature is the verbose mode, enabled with the -v or --verbose option. This prints the execution time for each test that is run. This— combined with being able to run a specific test file—can help you discover any particularly slow tests in your test suite.

For example:

```
$ rails test test/controllers/todos_controller_test.rb -v
```

```
Run options: -v --seed 38407

# Running:

TodosControllerTest#test_should_get_index = 0.09 s = .

TodosControllerTest#test_should_destroy_todo = 0.02 s = .

TodosControllerTest#test_should_create_todo = 0.01 s = .

TodosControllerTest#test_should_show_todo = 0.00 s = .

TodosControllerTest#test_should_update_todo = 0.01 s = .

Finished in 0.139012s, 35.9682 runs/s, 50.3554 assertions/s.

5 runs, 7 assertions, 0 failures, 0 errors, 0 skips
```

▓ **Note** If you wish to keep an eye on the performance of your tests, you should take a look at the minitest-profile gem. With it installed, using the --profile option will list the ten slowest tests at the end of each run. You can learn more at https://github.com/nmeans/minitest-profile.

Run Tests by Name

Another feature of MiniTest that is often overlooked (and which is now included in the test runner) is the ability to run tests by name. This -n option allows you to specify a regular expression and any tests that match this are executed. Again, this can really help with test development and debugging.

Remember, because you are passing in a RegEx, if you require matching a test name on something other than an exact match, you need to surround the search string with /. For example:

```
$ rails test -n /show/
```

```
Run options: -n /show/ --seed 35219

# Running:

.

Finished in 0.135740s, 7.3670 runs/s, 7.3670 assertions/s.

1 runs, 1 assertions, 0 failures, 0 errors, 0 skips
```

You can also specify a string with the –n argument, but this string must be an exact match with the test that you wish to run, so it's much more commonly used with regular expressions.

Fail Fast

Another great feature of the test runner is the option to fail fast. This mode is enabled with the -f or --fail-fast option.

When enabled, the execution of the test suite is aborted as soon as a test failure is encountered. If you have a test suite that takes a long time to run, this could save you some time.

Colored Test Output

One last hint: you can produce a colored output by specifying the -p or --pride flag.

Controller Request Named Parameters

Rails 5 brings a simple but welcome change to the helper methods used for the HTTP request tests in controller tests.

In previous versions of Rails, the get, post, put, patch, delete, and head methods took the name of the controller action to call, followed by a number of options arguments: request parameters, session variables, and flash values. But these optional values always had to be in that order, and if you wanted to omit one, you had to use a nil value.

For example, to call a get method with no parameters but with a flash message, you would have to use this:

```
get :index, nil, nil, { message: "Welcome" }
```

The multiple `nil` arguments present in the statement make the request confusing to read and it's all too easy to miss a nil when writing tests.

Rails 5 allows you to pass in these optional arguments as keyword arguments, so the preceding request would be rewritten as follows:

```
get :index, flash: { message: "Welcome" }
```

To simulate a request with parameters, use the `params` keyword:

```
post :create, params: { name: "Fred" }
```

You can use the keywords `params`, `session`, `flash`, `body`, `xhr`, and `format` with the HTTP test helpers, as can be seen in the following examples:

```
get :show, params: { id: 31 },
           session: { user_id: 9 },
           format: :json

post :create, params: { user: { name: "Fred" } },
             flash: { message: "User created" }
```

This also means that the `xhr` helper has been removed in favor of using the `xhr` keyword. So, for instance,

```
xhr :post, :create, params: { name: 'Alan' }
```

becomes

```
post :create, params: { name: 'Alan' }, xhr: true
```

The use of keyword arguments makes your tests clearer and easier to read and understand.

For the moment, the old-style still works, but it's likely that it will be deprecated in the future, so it's worth moving to the new syntax for new tests.

Deprecation of assert_template and assigns

If you are already using MiniTest and have a comprehensive test suite, one change that is likely to affect you is that the controller test assertions `assert_template` and `assigns` have been deprecated.

Depending on how you previously approached testing controllers, this may or may not be concerning, but in my experience, a lot of teams rely heavily on both of these in their controller tests.

The reasoning behind the removal of both of these is mainly due to an evolution of how the Rails core team believes controller testing should be done. Controller tests should be concerned with what the responses of the controller methods are, not the internal details of how the response was created.

assert_template and assigns are both used to test implementation details rather than what is actually produced as a result of the request. If a view is abstracted into partials, then any assert_template tests are likely to break, even though the end response is the same. Which instance variables are set through the use of assigns should not be a concern of your test.

A controller test should be testing the following:

- That the HTTP status code is correct

- That the rendered output contains the correct data and DOM elements

- Changes to the persisted data

So, rather than checking that an instance variable was set, you should use assert_select to check if the expected data is present in the rendered output. This output may be HTML, but the same applies to testing an API response in JSON, in which case the JSON response would be parsed and the expected data matched.

It could be debated that this style of testing is much closer to an integration test than a unit test for a controller; that is, we are testing a request from beginning to end, ensuring all of the pieces are working together. In fact, David Heinemeier Hansson has suggested that in the future, Rails may move to favor integration tests over controller tests.

Integration tests in earlier versions of Rails tended to be slow to run, but as a result of the performance improvements in Rails 5, this is no longer an issue.

▩ **Note** If you absolutely must continue to use assert_template and assigns, then you can simply use the rails-controller-testing gem, which restores the functionality. The homepage for the extracted implementation is at https://github.com/rails/rails-controller-testing.

This change also affects RSpec, since it expects both of the assertions to be available. At the time of writing, the RSpec project is planning to automatically include the rails-controller-testing gem, if necessary.

Fixtures

Although a lot of people prefer to use factories for creating model data for their test cases, fixtures are still a very fast, simple, and powerful way to create model test data. The release of Rails 5 comes with a few nice enhancements to fixtures.

Fixture Model Class

There is now an optional special key settable in a fixture file to specify the model class name. So if you are using a database table that is named something different from a pluralized version of the class name, you can specify it using the following:

```
_fixture:
  model_class: User
alan:
  name: Alan
```

This was possible in earlier versions by using set_fixture_class within the test case class itself. However, since this setting is related to the fixture rather than the test case, and having it set in the test case precludes fixtures being properly loaded by the task db:fixtures:load, this fixture's metadata has been moved into the fixture file itself.

The old method isn't marked for deprecation just yet, but if you make use of this feature, it's probably a good idea to start using this method instead.

Enum Values

Enums are a sometimes overlooked feature of Active Record, allowing you to use integer database columns to represent a fixed set of values for a model attribute.

Previously, if you used enum attributes in your model, when creating a fixture for that model, you had to use the equivalent integer value of the required value of the enum attribute. This made the fixtures less readable resulting in wasted time having to refer back to the enum definition.

Rails 5 allows you to use a symbol or a string of the enum value rather than the integer representing that value.

For instance, your model defines an enum attribute as follows:

```
enum :language, [:english, :french]
```

Whereas previously, you would have to know that english is the first enum value, therefore having the value 0, you can now write the fixture as follows:

```
fred:
  name: Fred
  language: :english
```

Request via Redirect Deprecation

Another deprecation in Rails 5 is a change to the integration test helpers.

In Rails 5, the request_via_redirect integration request helper and all of the associated methods for each of the HTTP request methods (such as post_via_redirect) have been removed. This method was most often used to allow you to perform requests such as `post_via_redirect` or `patch_via_redirect`, which performed the request and then followed any subsequent redirects. Since that is a reasonably common behavior for web applications after a POST or PATCH request, it is often found in integration tests.

Thankfully, it is a simple change to continue testing this. All you need to do is perform the desired HTTP request and then manually call `follow_redirect!` directly afterward.

Summary

Although there are no revolutionary changes to the testing framework in Rails 5, the attention given to the Test Runner is very welcome and the overall performance improvements, especially in integration tests, make a big difference in day-to-day development.

The improvements to fixtures also make life easier in certain cases for more complex applications.

The deprecation of `assert_template` and `assigns` is an indicator of both the thinking of the Rails core team and the direction that the test framework may be headed in. It's definitely worth considering these changes and how they may affect the way that you design your tests.

CHAPTER 5

Rails API

While Rails is generally used to develop web-based applications, the increasing requirement to build API-only services has resulted in many people using Rails to build apps that have no web front end at all.

While this is certainly possible, it means that there are often a lot of unused gems and middleware overhead, slowing it down and getting in the way.

In order to make API application development simpler, Rails 5 has merged the Rails API project into Rails.

Using Rails for API Servers

Back in 2004 when Rails was first released to the world, the connected world was a very different place.

Very few web sites offered API access, and those that did usually exposed the API using SOAP, XML-RPC, CORBA, or their own unique quirky API protocol. There was no common consensus on authentication methods, so some allowed tokenized access and some relied on HTTP Basic. The output of the APIs was usually XML.

While both the RESTful architecture style and JSON as an output format had been around for many years, neither had yet been universally adopted by the web development community.

The majority of mobile phones had small 128×128 pixel displays, 3G rollout was still in the very early stages (and the corresponding data allowances were tiny and expensive) and most mobile application development was limited to small J2ME applications with limited functionality. Therefore, the developer demand for APIs was still small.

Web applications all used the traditional full-page reload for each request and use of JavaScript was limited to small, snippets of functionality.

However, obviously, a lot has changed since then. The use of connected devices has grown astronomically in the last decade, meaning your application is likely to require an API for iOS and Android applications. It is now common to be requested to build a purely API-driven application that has no web interface at all, both to serve as back ends for mobile and desktop apps. Advances in JavaScript mean that it's now possible to build highly interactive, complex browser interfaces that purely use the server via an API rather than relying on traditional HTML server responses. Also, the rise in adoption of microservice architectures means that more than ever, Rails is being used to build API-only applications.

© Alan Bradburne 2016
A. Bradburne, *Rails 5 Revealed*, DOI 10.1007/978-1-4842-1709-2_5

Rails has long provided ways of allowing creation of APIs, but with the inclusion of the Rails API project into Rails itself, there is now a standardized way of doing this.

The Rails API Project

The Rails API project started in 2012 as a gem that provided a way to generate a Rails application excluding parts of the framework that aren't necessary to create an application with no HTML front end. Over time, it kept up with the Rails releases, became more configurable and now, with the release of Rails 5, has been merged and become part of the framework itself.

JSON Response Creation

By default, a Rails 5 API-only application just relies on the to_json method of each model to generate the JSON output, but you will likely want to make use of a serialization library such as JBuilder or Active Model Serializers.

In this book, we will look at the Active Model Serializers gem. The Active Model Serializers library was part of the Rails API project and was originally planned to be the default for Rails 5 API applications, but this was changed in the Rails 5 beta releases and now it ships with no default library.

Active Model Serializers

Active Model Serializers (often referred to as AMS) allows you to easily create serializers for Active Model objects, encapsulating all of the serializer logic for each model. Out of the box, Active Model Serializer understands Active Model objects and it follows the Rails convention of using current_user for the authenticated user object. Because of this, creating JSON or XML serializers for APIs is made elegant and simple.

Most interestingly, maybe, is the support of the JSON API adapter. The JSON API project is an attempt at creating a standard convention for JSON API responses. This includes standard syntax for embedding related objects, links to other objects and pagination links. AMS allows different adapters to be used, so use of the JSON API adapter is not mandatory; by default, a simple attributes adapter is used.

While there are a vast number of alternative JSON serializer projects, AMS has gained a huge following and has become the preferred solution for a large number of developers.

JSON API

If you've ever built an API as part of a team, you'll likely be familiar with the amount of time going back and forth between server and client developers about how the API should function, the format of the JSON responses, how pagination should work, if you should use IDs or URLs to resources, etc.

JSON API is a specification for how a modern JSON API should work, based on experience of building real-world applications. By defining a clear and sensible set of guidelines, developers can spend less time debating the API format and more time building the application.

The JSON API specification was originally designed by Yehuda Katz who designed the specification originally as part of the Ember framework (a JavaScript web application framework). He wanted to define a standard format to allow backend applications to be compatible with Ember applications running client-side.

Since, at the time, Rails applications with APIs tended to have interfaces that were RESTful, but didn't adhere to any particular standard, he decided to create his own.

That project gained adoption outside of Ember and version 1.0 of the JSON API specification was released in May 2015.

There are libraries available for many platforms and languages that allow client and server developers to easily implement a JSON API compatible API.

You can read more about the JSON API specification at http://jsonapi.org/ and see a list of the available implementations at http://jsonapi.org/implementations/.

Why Use Rails for an API Application?

If you are considering building an API-only application, you may automatically consider a framework such as Sinatra or Grape, because people often consider Rails too heavy for an API app.

However, if you've ever done just this, unless your application is very simple, you often find that you end up having to reimplement features that are provided by the framework in a Rails app. Features like having built-in support for live reloading; providing different environments for development, testing, and production; simple routing; URL generation; and parameter parsing. Of course, Rails also provides great security support and authentication features.

Plus, if you are already familiar with building applications in Rails, it's incredibly convenient to be able to use the same tools that you already know well.

So, yes, while you certainly can use a smaller, lighter framework to write an API application, having the Rails tool set backing you up makes life a whole lot easier and allows you to be more productive.

Building an API Application

Let's go ahead and create an API-only Rails application. This is done using the usual rails new command, but with the addition of the --api option. For example:

```
$ rails new TodoApi --api
```

First, open up the project's Gemfile. You'll immediately notice that this is a lot lighter than the regular Gemfile generated for a new Rails application. All the gems related to web interfaces such as jQuery, CoffeeScript, and the asset pipeline are omitted.

As mentioned earlier, no serialization gems are included in the default Gemfile, so you should add the AMS gem and bundle install now:

```
gem 'active_model_serializers'
```

If you look at the generated Application Controller at app/controllers/application_controller.rb (as shown in Listing 5-1), you'll see that that class inherits from ActionController::API (rather than the usual ActionController::Base)

Listing 5-1. The Generated API Application Controller

```
class ApplicationController < ActionController::API
end
```

This class definition is also missing the protect_from_forgery statement that is usually included, which is used to detect CSRF attacks. Since this only relates to web forms, it is not necessary for an API-only application.

If you take a look at the generated config/application.rb file, you'll see the following option:

```
config.api_only = true
```

As discussed earlier, this limits what middleware is loaded. Some of the middleware that is excluded are things like cookies, sessions, and flash messaging. If you require any of these in your application, you can always reenable them by using, for example:

```
config.middleware.use ActionDispatch::Cookies
```

could be added to your config/application.rb file.

Also, you'll notice that where the application.rb file usually contains the statement require 'rails/all', the API application lists the individual frameworks that are loaded, allowing you finer control over while parts of Rails are required for you application.

You may have noticed that the generated application is missing the directories app/assets, app/helpers, and app/views. Since these directories are all related to applications with web interfaces, they are simply omitted from any apps generated with the Rails API option.

So now that we know our way around the generated application, let's create a simple API-only project. I will use a simple to-do application as an example, where a todo model will have title and a completed at timestamp.

We can use the rails generate command in the same was as we would for a regular Rails application. Using generate scaffold:

```
$ rails g scaffold todo title completed_at:timestamp
```

invoke	active_record
create	db/migrate/20151012134203_create_todos.rb
create	app/models/todo.rb
invoke	test_unit
create	test/models/todo_test.rb
create	test/fixtures/todos.yml
invoke	resource_route
route	resources :todos
create	app/serializers/todo_serializer.rb
invoke	scaffold_controller
create	app/controllers/todos_controller.rb
invoke	test_unit
create	test/controllers/todos_controller_test.rb

This generated code is a fully working API application. Let's take a look at what was generated and how it differs from a traditional Rails app.

The generated migration and model, model test file and addition to the routes.rb file are exactly the same as those that would be created for a normal Rails web application. However, the controller, serializer, and controller test files are rather different than if we ran the generator without the api_only setting enabled. Also, you'll note that there are no view files, as the only output of our application will be created by specifying a response in your code or calling the relevant serializers.

Let's look at the generated serializer. It is shown in Listing 5-2.

Listing 5-2. The Generated TodoSerializer

```
class TodoSerializer < ActiveModel::Serializer
  attributes :id, :title, :completed_at
end
```

As you might expect, this means that the object is serialized by including the attribute's id, title, and completed_at values.

You can extensively customize the output of the serializer. Naturally, you can remove any attributes from this list if, say, there are fields used internally that shouldn't be exposed via the API. You can also add additional attributes that are method calls on the object, or are just methods within the object's serializer class.

For example, if we wished to add a Boolean attribute called completed, we could do this by adding a completed instance method to either the model or the serializer and then adding this attribute to the list in the serializer definition, as shown in Listing 5-3.

Listing 5-3. Example of a TodoSerializer with a Custom Attribute

```
class TodoSerializer < ActiveModel::Serializer
  attributes :id, :title, :completed_at
  attributes :completed

  def completed
    completed_at.present?
  end
end
```

You can change the name of an attribute by specifying the key for a particular attribute. For example, we could change the name of the completed_at attribute to be finished_at in the output by changing the serialization attributes as shown in Listing 5-4.

Listing 5-4. Example of TodoSerializer with a Renamed Attribute

```
class TodoSerializer < ActiveModel::Serializer
  attributes :id, :title
  attribute :completed_at, key: :finished_at
end
```

It is also possible to embed associations within the JSON output by simply adding has_many (or has_one) and belongs_to to the relevant serializers. For example, if our application had a notes model, and each todo item could have one or more notes, you could include the relevant notes within the JSON output for a todo item by adding a has_many statement to the serializer as shown in Listing 5-5.

Listing 5-5. Example of TodoSerializer with Embedded Notes

```
class TodoSerializer < ActiveModel::Serializer
  attributes :id, :title, :completed_at
  has_many :notes
end
```

Let's now take a look at the controller created by the scaffold generator, shown in Listing 5-6.

Listing 5-6. The Scaffold Generated TodosController

```
class TodosController < ApplicationController
  before_action :set_todo, only: [:show, :update, :destroy]

  # GET /todos
  def index
    @todos = Todo.all

    render json: @todos
  end
```

```
  # GET /todos/1
  def show
    render json: @todo
  end

  # POST /todos
  def create
    @todo = Todo.new(todo_params)

    if @todo.save
      render json: @todo, status: :created, location: @todo
    else
      render json: @todo.errors, status: :unprocessable_entity
    end
  end

  # PATCH/PUT /todos/1
  def update
    if @todo.update(todo_params)
      render json: @todo
    else
      render json: @todo.errors, status: :unprocessable_entity
    end
  end

  # DELETE /todos/1
  def destroy
    @todo.destroy
  end

  private
    # Use callbacks to share common setup or constraints between actions.
    def set_todo
      @todo = Todo.find(params[:id])
    end

    # Only allow a trusted parameter "white list" through.
    def todo_params
      params.require(:todo).permit(:title, :completed_at, :position)
    end
end
```

You may notice some interesting differences from the controllers you are used to seeing generated by Rails. First, each action has a render json: statement rather than relying on Rails to find the relevant view file.

Next, there are no "edit" or "new" actions in the controller. This is because in a pure API application there is simply no need for these requests. An HTML based web application requires new and edit actions to provide users with a form that allows them to enter and submit data to the server's create and update actions respectively. In an API, the API client can just access those methods directly with no need for a form.

Another interesting thing to note is that the render methods called in the create action includes both a status and location in the response, along with returning the created object as JSON (which is of course defined by the serializer). This is the expected behavior for a RESTful API: the 201 Created HTTP status is returned, the URI for the created resource is returned in the HTTP headers and the created resource in the body.

Let's spin up the application and look at how it responds.

Perform the pending database migrations with this:

```
$ rails db:migrate
```

And then start the server with this:

```
$ rails s
```

Now we can attempt some API requests using cURL:

```
$ curl -H "Content-Type:application/json" -X POST -d '{"todo":{"title":
"Write a book"}}' http://localhost:3000/todos
```

```
{
  "id": 1,
  "title": "Write a book",
  "completed_at": null
}
```

> **Note** I have formatted the response from cURL as to make it easier to read. When manually testing and investigating APIs, I'd highly recommend using a tool such as Postman for Chrome (https://www.getpostman.com) or Paw for OS X (https://luckymarmot.com/paw).

Note that since we are sending the data as JSON rather than a form post or as URL parameters, we need to set the Content-Type header to application/json. Without this, Rails will not correctly parse the data sent with the request.

The response to a POST from the controllers from by the scaffold generator is to return the object just created. This is generally good practice so stick with this unless you have a specific use case. Returning the created resource is important so that the client can confirm that all the values have been stored correctly, if any additional values have been set by the server, if any values have been transformed, and importantly, inform the client of the id of the object. Obviously, you can change this response behavior in the controller.

Now that we have created a todo item, we can retrieve the list of objects via the index method.

```
$ curl http://localhost:3000/todos
```

```
[
  {

    "id":1,

    "title":"Write a book",

    "completed_at":null

  }

]
```

As expected, an array is returned with each item listing the attributes, which are listed in the TodoSerializer. As described earlier, you can add, remove, or transform attributes from there.

Active Model Serializer Adapters

Earlier, I mentioned that Active Model Serializer uses adapters to describe how the attributes and object relationships should be serialized, therefore providing support for different styles of API responses. Let's look at how these can be used and affect the output.

By default, Active Model Serializers use AttributesAdapter, which is a very simple adapter that provides basic JSON serialization, but without a root key. If you require a root key in the JSON output, you can use the alternative JsonAdapter.

To do this, create a new initializer called config/initializers/api_adaptor.rb containing the following line:

```
ActiveModel::Serializer.config.adapter = :json
```

Restart your Rails server and retry the cURL index request. The returned JSON will
be as follows:

```
{
  "todos": [
    {
      "id": 1,
      "title": "Write a book",
      "completed_at": null
    }
  ]
}
```

Now, the root key of the returned object is the name of the object's class.

However, this is still a pretty limited API implementation, since you still have to
decide on, adopt, and implement other specifics of your API, such as how pagination
works, how errors are returned, and how related and nested objects work.

As discussed earlier, the JSON API specification aims to improve this situation
by describing how an ideal API should work in regards to things like pagination and
relationships.

Active Model Serializer includes an adapter called JsonApiAdapter, which helps
you easily implement an API that conforms to the JSON API specification. The Active
Model Serializer gem developers recommend the use of the JSON API adapter over the
basic attributes adapter or JSON adapter because it is the most fully featured and actively
developed adapter. Obviously, depending on your application requirements, using the
JSON API standard may not be possible for you, but if you are building a greenfield API,
you should strongly consider it.

So, let's make a few changes to the app. First, enable the JsonApiAdapter by changing
the config/initializers/api_adapter.rb to the following:

```
ActiveModel::Serializer.config.adapter = :json_api
```

Now, let's add pagination to the index request. The AMS JsonApiAdapter supports
both Kaminari and WillPaginate gems. In this example, I'll use Kaminari. Add the gem to
your Gemfile as follows:

```
gem 'kaminari'
```

Then perform a bundle install.

The JSON API specification recommends that servers use the page parameter
name for pagination operations, so we will use page[number] for the page number and
page[size] for the number of items per page. Since Kaminari sets a default if a nil page
number and page size is passed, we can simply change our TodoController index method
as shown in Listing 5-7.

Listing 5-7. The TodoController Index Method with Pagination

```
def index
  if params[:page]
    page_number = params[:page][:number]
    size = params[:page][:size]
  end

  @todos = Todo.page(page_number).per(size)

  render json: @todos
end
```

If no page parameter is supplied at all, both the page number and the page size are set to the default.

After restarting the server to pick up the initializer change, reload the todo index. To make the pagination examples clearer, I have added some additional todo items.

```
$ curl http://localhost:3000/todos
```

```
{
  "data": [
    {
      "id": "1",
      "type": "todos",
      "attributes": {
        "title": "Write a book",
        "completed_at": null
      }
    },
    {
      "id": "2",
      "type": "todos",
      "attributes": {
        "title": "eat dinner",
        "completed_at": null
      }
    },
```

```
    {
      "id": "3",
      "type": "todos",
      "attributes": {
        "title": "walk the dog",
        "completed_at": null
      }
    }
  ],
  "links": {}
}
```

You'll notice that the output is rather different from the simple JSON adapters we used earlier. Following the JSON API specification, rather than having the root key as the resource name, or simply nothing, it has the key data. Then, the resource data lists the id, the type (i.e., the name of the resource object), and attributes as the attributes of the resource.

To see the effect of adding pagination and how the links appear, repeat the index call with a small page size and on the second page, as follows:

```
$ curl --globoff http://localhost:3000/todos?page[size]=1&page[number]=2
```

```
{
  "data": [
    {
      "id": "2",
      "type": "todos",
      "attributes": {
        "title": "eat dinner",
        "completed_at": null
      }
    }
```

```
    ],
    "links": {
        "self": "http://localhost:3000/todos?page%5Bnumber%5D=2&page%5Bsize%5D=1",
        "first": "http://localhost:3000/todos?page%5Bnumber%5D=1&page%5Bsize%5D=1",
        "prev": "http://localhost:3000/todos?page%5Bnumber%5D=1&page%5Bsize%5D=1",
        "next": "http://localhost:3000/todos?page%5Bnumber%5D=3&page%5Bsize%5D=1",
        "last": "http://localhost:3000/todos?page%5Bnumber%5D=3&page%5Bsize%5D=1"
    }
}
```

░ **Note**   In the previous cURL example, it was necessary to use the option `--globoff` because, otherwise, the characters [and] are interpreted by cURL itself and the command fails. This option disables the "URL globbing parser" for cURL.

The links hash has values for self, first, prev, next, and last. The client application can then step through the pages as necessary.

If an object has relationships and they are specified in the serializers, the related object types and ids will be detailed in the JSON API response. For instance, if our todo items could have multiple notes added to them, our TodoSerializer would look as shown in Listing 5-8.

Listing 5-8. Adding a Relationship to the TodoSerializer

```
class TodoSerializer < ActiveModel::Serializer
  attributes :id, :title, :completed_at
  has_many :notes
end
```

A NoteSerializer would detail the reciprocal relationship, as shown in Listing 5-9.

Listing 5-9. The NoteSerializer Class

```
class NoteSerializer < ActiveModel::Serializer
  attributes :body
  belongs_to :todo
end
```

Now, a request for the detail of a todo object includes a relationships key, as shown here:

```
{
  "data": {
    "id": "1",
    "type": "todos",
    "attributes": {
      "title": "Write a book",
      "completed_at": null
    },
    "relationships": {
      "notes": {
        "data": [
          {
            "id": "1",
            "type": "notes"
          }
        ]
      }
    }
  }
}
```

However, this currently means that the client would have to perform a separate request to get the detail on the note with id 1.

AMS also supports nested resources. This is a very useful feature to allow clients to request documents with related objects included in the JSON response. Depending on how the data is structured and how the client application works, the client may be able to perform fewer API requests to present the necessary data.

If we wished to include all related notes objects in our response, we can add the include argument to the render statement, as follows:

```
render json: @todo, include: 'notes'
```

This would result in the following response:

```
{
  "data": {
    "id": "1",
    "type": "todos",
    "attributes": {
      "title": "Write a book",
      "completed_at": null
    },
    "relationships": {
      "notes": {
        "data": [
          {
            "id": "1",
            "type": "notes"
          }
        ]
      }
    }
  },
  "included": [
    {
      "id": "1",
      "type": "notes",
      "attributes": {
        "body": "this is important"
      },
```

```
    "relationships": {
      "todo": {
        "data": {
          "id": "1",
          "type": "todos"
        }
      }
    }
  }
]
}
```

Now the client can match up the related note with the respective todo object.

The include argument can be either a string or an array; AMS parses it as necessary. As suggested by the JSON API spec, you can request an include nesting associated object too; for example, if you were rendering a number of items, you could include the associated review objects and the author objects associated with those reviews, as follows:

```
render @items, include: 'reviews,reviews.author'
```

Obviously, this may potentially result in some queries taking longer than required, so consider this carefully.

You can also use a wild card option (*), which includes the immediately associated objects; ** recursively includes all nested objects. Again, this could very well cause some performance issues if implemented carelessly.

Since AMS accepts a string, it is possible to just pass params[:include] to the render statement; however, you should never do this without carefully considering the implications of a user requesting a recursive wildcard. Filter and sanitize as necessary!

Caching

Active Model Serializers also support the caching of responses. It uses the configured Rails cache store in the same way as view caching works.

To enable caching, simply add the cache statement to a serializer and specify a key that will be used to generate the cache key.

To demonstrate this, let's leave the development cache store as the default "memory store," and enable caching in development mode with the following command:

```
$ rails dev:cache
```

```
Development mode is now being cached.
```

You must restart your rails server to pick up the change to cache configuration. The server must also be started with the -C or --dev-caching options to allow the server to use a cache in development mode.

Now enable caching responses of the Todo serializer by adding the cache statement to the serializer class (see Listing 5-10).

Listing 5-10. Adding Caching to the TodoSerializer

```
class TodoSerializer < ActiveModel::Serializer
  cache key: 'todo', expires_in: 24.hours
  attributes :id, :title, :completed_at
  has_many :notes
end
```

As each todo object response is initially rendered, it is cached with the key "todo/#{todo.id}-#{todo.updated_at}". Since the updated_at timestamp is part of the key, this means that the key is changed whenever the object is updated. This means that we don't need to worry about manually expiring the object at all. In this example, I've set the optional cache setting expires_in so that the cached data is automatically expired after one day.

It is also possible to partially cache objects by specifying only or except arguments to the cache statement. For example, if you only wished to cache the title attribute of each todo item, you would change the serializer cache statement to this:

```
cache key: 'todo', expires_in: 24.hours, only: [:title]
```

When planning your API application caching strategy, you should also consider using supporting HTTP conditional GETs using the ETag or Last-Modified headers. These are described in the official Rails caching guide at http://guides.rubyonrails.org/caching_with_rails.html.

Summary

In this chapter, you looked at how Rails API provides an alternative generated application, allowing you to easily build an API-only application.

By using this generator option, you get a slimmed-down Rails application that is optimized for developing API-only applications. By using Active Model Serializers, you are able to easily create APIs that adhere to the JSON API specification.

CHAPTER 6

Action Cable

Action Cable is one of the most exciting features of Rails 5. Action Cable allows you to easily add real-time, full-duplex communication to you Rails application, allowing us to build pages that are updated dynamically.

Action Cable uses the WebSocket protocol to enable our server to send real-time messages to individual users or broadcast messages to all currently online users. It provides a very "Rails-like" interface for the entire WebSocket front-end and back-end code, making it very easy for existing Rails developers to add functionality that was previously complex or simply not possible with just Rails.

WebSocket

Before we get into the details of Action Cable, let's first look at the underlying technology: WebSocket.

Up until now, all Rails applications have made use of HTTP. You will no doubt be very familiar with how this works, but just to reiterate, this means that the Rails application accepts HTTP requests (usually via a web server such as Apache or NGINX), processes the request, and returns a response. Hopefully, this will take no more than a few hundred milliseconds. Depending on your choice of Rails web server (i.e., Puma, Unicorn, etc.) and how your environment is configured, your application will only have a handful of open and active communications channels at any one time.

WebSocket presents a very different way of communicating between your application and the client's browser. The WebSocket protocol is a full-duplex communication channel between your application and the user's browser. This connection uses TCP and runs over port 80, the same as HTTP, but the way it works is very different.

Rather than requiring the client to initiate separate HTTP requests each time that it wishes to send or receive data, it opens a connection to the server that stays open for the duration of the session—that is, until the user navigates away from the page or closes the browser tab.

Once the connection is open, both the server and the client can exchange messages at any time, irrespective of user input. On the client side, you write JavaScript code to execute when a WebSocket message is received, on the server side, Action Cable allows you to write Ruby methods to handle received messages in a very similar way that you would process a HTTP request.

© Alan Bradburne 2016
A. Bradburne, *Rails 5 Revealed*, DOI 10.1007/978-1-4842-1709-2_6

The WebSocket protocol uses ws:// and wss:// prefixes to indicate insecure and secure WebSocket connections, respectively.

Architecture of an Action Cable Application

A Rails app that involves an Action Cable component is a little more complicated than a traditional HTTP request-response application.

First, there is the main Rails application itself. This is no different from any normal Rails application. It's possible to add Action Cable feature to any Rails application once it has been updated to Rails 5.

The Action Cable specific code is then separated into app/channels for the back-end Ruby code and app/assets/javascripts/channels for the client-side JavaScript or CoffeeScript code.

While it is certainly possible to go crazy and build your entire application around WebSocket connections, it is designed for and works best when the functionality is added selectively to parts of your application that require this kind of feature.

Pub/Sub

Action Cable is based around the Publish-Subscribe messaging pattern, often referred to as Pub/Sub or simply pubsub. This is exactly as it sounds: it allows a publisher (in our case, the Action Cable part of your Rails application) to publish "messages" via a channel to any subscribers (in our case, the client browsers that are subscribed to the relevant channels.). Clients can subscribe and unsubscribe to channels as necessary and only receive messages for the channels they are subscribed to.

Connections

When a browser loads a page that you have enabled Action Cable on, it will attempt to open a "connection" with the Action Cable server.

For each incoming WebSocket connection, the server instantiates an Action Cable connection object that is used to authenticate and identify the user if necessary. This instance becomes the parent of all the channel subscriptions for that client to the Action Cable server. The connection itself only deals with authentication and authorization.

This connection code is specified in app/channels/connection.rb and there will generally be only one Connection class per application.

Channels

Your client-side application only opens one Action Cable connection to the server, but then can subscribe to a number of channels via this connection. It can then use each of these channels to send and receive messages to the server.

In your Rails Action Cable server code, you define a number of channel classes. Each channel should be used to communicate a particular specified activity or type of event. For example, you may use CommentsChannel to listen for and display new comments are they are created, or OnlineStatusChannel to listen for users coming online or going offline to update an on-screen list.

Since the WebSocket Connection class is bidirectional, your client application can use these channels to listen for incoming messages and transmit messages back to the Action Cable server.

Rails 5 WebSocket Implementation Details

In order to enable a WebSocket application to be built using Rails, Action Cable makes use of a number of other dependencies. In particular, it requires a subscription service and a Rails application server to handle the WebSocket requests.

In the initial versions of Action Cable, Redis was the only supported Pub/Sub server, but now many different types of adapters ship with Action Cable, including support for asynchronous, inline, PostgreSQL, evented Redis, and non-evented Redis.

You can use the same Rails application server for both your core Rails application and also the Action Cable server, but while this is definitely suitable for using during development and for deployment of smaller sites, you may wish to consider using a separate application server processes for the main web application and the Action Cable server. This will allow you to monitor and tweak each separately to handle the load specific to your site.

Pub/Sub Back End

Action Cable requires a Pub/Sub service to be available for use as the back-end messaging system. At the time of writing, Action Cable supports Redis and PostgreSQL, along with asynchronous and inline adapters.

You may have come across Redis before and quite possibly used it in a Rails application as it is commonly used as the backing for Rails cache storage, but it also features a very fast and stable implementation of Pub/Sub.

PostgreSQL 9.1 introduced a Pub/Sub system that can also be utilized for Action Cable. Since the back-end services are abstracted with adapters, you can easily change the back-end service and test to find out which performs better for your requirements.

The Async and Inline adapters are designed for use in development mode, allowing you to use the same Rails server as the Action Cable server.

Building a Chat Application

To demonstrate how Action Cable can be used in a real-world Rails application, we will build a simple chat application. We will initially build a traditional Rails application and then change the app to feature a live message list where the page is immediately updated with new messages as they are posted.

Application Specification

To properly demonstrate, the supporting application will be a simple Rails application with two models:

- User

- Message

The user model will store the user's name. We will save this in a database table. We will just use the default SQLite database for this application.

The message model will store all the chat message content, along with the user_id of the corresponding author of each message. Again, we will use SQLite to store this to keep the code as simple as possible in demonstrating the Action Cable features.

By storing all the users and messages in a database table, when a new user comes to the site, they will be presented with all the messages that have been posted up to that point.

In order to simplify the application, I won't build any authentication, just a simple sign-in page that either creates a new user record or updates an existing one, indexed on the given username.

The initial version of the app will not use Action Cable, once we have the working traditional application, we will modify it to make use of WebSocket.

Create the Basic Application

Although Action Cable is delivered as a separate gem, it is included by default for new Rails 5 applications.

Create the application using the normal Rails application generator:

```
$ rails new livechat
```

If you look at the freshly created application, you notice some additions to the usual Rails project skeleton.

First, there is a new directory called channels within app/. This directory contains your Ruby code for the server-side component of your Action Cable feature, such as accepting and authenticating requests, processing incoming messages, and specifying what data to send out to the clients.

There is a new config file within config/ called cable.yml. As you can likely guess, this contains the configuration for the Action Cable back end, currently Redis or PostgreSQL.

There is also a new directory within assets/javascripts/, called cable. This contains the JavaScript client-side component of your code, which contains the WebSocket connection code, along with detailing what channels to subscribe to and what actions to take on incoming messages on those channels. By default, Rails generates CoffeeScript files rather than JavaScript.

Before we crack on with the Action Cable code, let's quickly create the simplest possible Rails app to support our features.

Users and Messages Resources

Create User and Message resources; a user just has a name string, messages belong to a user and have a text message body:

```
$ rails g resource user name:string:uniq
```

```
invoke   active_record
create   db/migrate/20160108213846_create_users.rb
create   app/models/user.rb
...
route    resources :users
```

And now messages:

```
$ rails g resource message user:references body:text
```

```
invoke   active_record
create   db/migrate/20160108213918_create_messages.rb
create   app/models/message.rb
...
route    resources :messages
```

Now let's add the message relationship to the user model, app/models/user.rb:

```
class User < ApplicationRecord
  has_many :messages
end
```

The reciprocal belongs_to relationship in the message.rb file is already created by the generator so there is no need to add that manually.

Run the migrations. (Don't forget that we now use the rails command rather than rake!) Since we're just using the default SQLite driver for the database, we don't need to run a command to create the database.

```
$ rails db:migrate
```

```
== 20160108213846 CreateUsers: migrating =================================

  -- create_table(:users)

        -> 0.0011s

  -- add_index(:users, :name, {:unique=>true})

        -> 0.0006s

  == 20160108213846 CreateUsers: migrated (0.0017s) ======================

  == 20160108213918 CreateMessages: migrating ============================

  -- create_table(:messages)

        -> 0.0011s

  == 20160108213918 CreateMessages: migrated (0.0012s) ===================
```

Now let's add a couple of simple controller methods to allow us to log in or create a user. Edit the app/controllers/users_controller.rb file, as shown in Listing 6-1.

Listing 6-1. The Users Controller File

```ruby
class UsersController < ApplicationController
  def new
    @user = User.new
  end

  def create
    @user = User.find_or_initialize_by(name: params[:user][:name])
    if @user.save
      cookies.signed[:user_id] = @user.id
      redirect_to messages_path
    else
      render :new
    end
  end
end
```

This simply presents a user log in/sign up form and, on submission of a user's name, either creates the user record if the user doesn't already exists, or finds the user record by name.

We then set a signed cookie to be the id of this user. Using a signed cookie ensures that the value cannot be tampered with on the client's machine.

Now create the associated view file, the log in/sign up form as app/views/users/new.html.erb. Create the form, as shown in Listing 6-2.

Listing 6-2. The User Created and Login Form

```
<h1>Sign up or Log in</h1>
<%= form_for @user do |form| %>
  <%= form.text_field :name %>
  <%= form.submit 'Log in' %>
<% end %>
```

Before we add the code for the messages controller, we should add some support methods for authenticating the user from the cookie we set in the log in process.

Edit app/controllers/application_controller.rb and add the methods, as shown in Listing 6-3.

Listing 6-3. The Application Controller File

```
class ApplicationController < ActionController::Base
  # Prevent CSRF attacks by raising an exception.
  # For APIs, you may want to use :null_session instead.

  protect_from_forgery with: :exception

  helper_method :current_user

  def require_user
    redirect_to new_user_path unless current_user
  end

  def current_user
    @current_user = User.find_by id: cookies.signed[:user_id]
  end
end
```

Now, we can use these methods to build our messages controller. This just has two methods: index, to list all messages, and create, to add a new message.

Edit the file app/controllers/messages_controller.rb and add the before_action and the index and create methods, as shown in Listing 6-4.

Listing 6-4. The Messages Controller File

```
class MessagesController < ApplicationController
  before_action :require_user

  def index
    @messages = Message.all
  end
```

```
  def create
    @message = current_user.messages.create! body: params[:message][:body]
    redirect_to messages_path
  end
end
```

As discussed earlier, this initial version doesn't make use of WebSocket, just traditional HTTP POST request to create messages, which in turn redirects the user's browser back to the messages index page, such as how a typical web page would implement a form to create a record.

Now add the corresponding view, app/views/messages/index.html.erb, as shown in Listing 6-5.

Listing 6-5. The Basic Messages Index View

```
<h1>Chat room</h1>

<p>Your name: <%= current_user.name %></p>

<h2>Messages</h2>
<%= form_for :message do |form| %>
  <%= form.text_field :body %>
  <%= form.submit 'Send Message' %>
<% end %>

<ul id="messages">
<% @messages.each do |message| %>
  <%= render partial: 'message', object: message %>
<% end %>
</ul>
```

The message partial file, app/views/messages/_message.html.erb, which is referenced in Listing 6-5, is shown in Listing 6-6.

Listing 6-6. The Message Partial View

```
<li>
  <%= message.user.name %>: <%= message.body %>
</li>
```

Finally, let's set the application's default route to point to the log in page. Edit config/routes.rb and add the root route before the final end statement:

```
root 'users#new'
```

Obviously, this is a woefully incomplete application but it demonstrates how a Rails application would perform the business of presenting a form and accepting HTTP POST requests to create objects.

To check that this is all working, start the application with `rails server` and open two different browser applications, for example Safari and Chrome, and opening `http://localhost:3000` on each.

Log in to one browser as "Fred" and log in to the other as "Julie", and then enter some messages in both browser windows. Immediately, we can see a problem: when other users enter new messages, they don't show in our browser until we either reload the page or send a message of our own, which causes the page to reload.

Obviously, this is a limitation of web pages that we've come to know and work around as necessary. The most common way around this in Rails applications is to use polling, in which each browser repeatedly sends requests to the server asking if there are any new messages. Obviously, the vast majority of the time there will be no new messages, but the client must keep polling every few seconds to make sure there is nothing new.

Clearly, this is a suboptimal state of affairs. Not only does it mean that the server is going to have to be able to withstand the constant barrage of polling requests from client browsers, but there is naturally going to be a delay in the message being posted and the client polling the server to discover it. This naturally depends on the frequency of polling, but depending on the trade-off made by the developers, this will likely be, at best, a few seconds. This might not be too important for our little chat application, but it precludes certain types of apps being developed if they require more immediate updates.

WebSocket allows us to massively improve our chat application and provide immediate delivery of messages to all connected clients and completely does away with the need for polling. Action Cable makes this incredibly easy to do in Rails. Let's get to work.

Set Up Action Cable

As discussed earlier, Action Cable requires a back-end service. A number of different subscription server adapters ship with Action Cable. By default, Rails now uses the Async adapter for development and testing environments, and the Redis adapter for production environments.

Async and Inline adapters allow the rails server itself to work as the subscription back-end server, meaning you don't have to use an external server such as Redis. However, since this is only recommended in development mode and you will require either Redis or PostgreSQL for production mode, I will demonstrate here how to use Redis as the back-end server.

Redis Installation

Redis is very easy to install. Since the Redis source code doesn't depend on any libraries or frameworks (apart from the standard libc), it is very simple to build from source. If you would like to do this, follow the instructions at `http://redis.io/topics/quickstart`.

For the sake of simplicity, I will show how to install on Linux and OS X using the package management tools `apt` and `brew`.

Redis is not officially supported on Windows, but there is a fork maintained by Microsoft. You can find out more about this at https://github.com/MSOpenTech/redis. If using Windows, you may find it simpler to make use of the PostgreSQL pub/sub adapter as that may be simpler to set up.

OS X Installation

To install Redis on OS X, we will use Homebrew, a package manager for OS X. If you don't already use Homebrew, you should read about it and follow the install instructions at http://brew.sh.

After Homebrew is installed and set up, install Redis with the command:

```
$ brew install redis
```

```
==> Downloading https://homebrew.bintray.com/bottles/redis-3.0.7.el_
capitan.bottle.1.tar.gz

Already downloaded: /Library/Caches/Homebrew/redis-3.0.7.el_capitan.
bottle.1.tar.gz

==> Pouring redis-3.0.7.el_capitan.bottle.1.tar.gz

==> Caveats

To have launchd start redis at login:

  ln -sfv /usr/local/opt/redis/*.plist ~/Library/LaunchAgents

Then to load redis now:

  launchctl load ~/Library/LaunchAgents/homebrew.mxcl.redis.plist

Or, if you don't want/need launchctl, you can just run:

  redis-server /usr/local/etc/redis.conf

==> Summary

/usr/local/Cellar/redis/3.0.7: 9 files, 876.3K
```

Follow the instructions and either set up Redis to start automatically, or just run with this:

```
$ redis-server /usr/local/etc/redis.conf
```

After successfully starting the server, you are presented with the message:

```
5620:M 18 Jan 23:04:25.805 # Server started, Redis version 3.0.7

5620:M 18 Jan 23:04:25.807 * DB loaded from disk: 0.003 seconds

5620:M 18 Jan 23:04:25.807 * The server is now ready to accept connections
on port 6379
```

Linux Installation

To install Redis on Linux, you can either follow the instructions at http://redis.io/
topics/quickstart to install from source, or install the apt package using

```
$ sudo apt-get -y install redis-server
```

```
Reading package lists... Done

Building dependency tree

...

Setting up redis-server (2:1.2.0-1) ...

Starting redis-server: redis-server.
```

This installs and automatically starts the Redis server.

Action Cable Configuration

The Action Cable back-end adapter configuration is set in the config/cable.yml
config file.

If you look at this file, you see that it follows the Rails convention of specifying
the different configurations for the application environments development, test, and
production. This config file is shown in Listing 6-7.

Listing 6-7. The Default Action Cable Back-end Configuration

```
# Action Cable uses Redis by default to administer connections, channels,
and sending/receiving messages over the WebSocket.
production:
  adapter: redis
  url: redis://localhost:6379/1
```

```
development:
  adapter: async

test:
  adapter: async
```

By default, Rails uses the Redis adapter for production and Async for development and test. As discussed earlier, we will change the development adapter to Redis to demonstrate how it is configured and used.

Change the development section of `config/cable.yml` to use Redis, as follows:

```
development:
  adapter: redis
  url: redis://localhost:6379/2
```

Action Cable Connection Setup

When each browser (or client application) first connects to our Action Cable server, they perform an HTTP request, which, in turn, opens a socket connection between the application running in the browser and our Action Cable server.

When your Rails application is created, a skeleton `Connection` class is defined in `app/channels/application_cable/connection.rb`. If you open this, you will see that it currently contains no methods, as shown in Listing 6-8.

Listing 6-8. The Generated ApplicationCable Class

```
# Be sure to restart your server when you modify this file. Action Cable
runs in an loop that does not support auto reloading.
module ApplicationCable
  class Connection < ActionCable::Connection::Base
  end
end
```

As mentioned earlier, in this connection class, we deal with any authentication logic to identify which user is initiating a WebSocket connection.

When the client application opens a WebSocket connection, as part of the handshake, it sends the same cookies that are used for a HTTP request, meaning that we receive any cookies that we have set elsewhere in our application.

As it is common Rails practice to save the user's id as a signed cookie on the client's machine, we can simply use this to identify the current logged-in user and load the user object in the same way as we would in a normal Rails authentication code.

Although the Action Cable code lives within the Rails app and has access to the model and view code, since it doesn't live within the usual Rails request life cycle, none of the application's `before_filters` are executed.

Instead, Action Cable `Connection` and `Channel` classes are expected to follow a set of conventions to match certain events, similar to the Rails callbacks that you already know.

When a connection attempt is made by the client, the method `connect` in the Connection class in the app/channels/application_cable/connection.rb file will be run. Similarly, the `disconnect` method will be executed when the WebSocket connection is severed (for instance, if the browser window is closed or the computer is powered down).

Within the connect method, we should perform any authentication and authorization that is necessary for any WebSocket channel. You also declare how this connection should be identified. Since we will be identifying a user by their id, we will use `current_user`.

So, let's go ahead and add the connection code to the `Connection` class, as shown in Listing 6-9.

Listing 6-9. Connection Class to Authenticate a User

```
module ApplicationCable
  class Connection < ActionCable::Connection::Base
    identified_by :current_user

    def connect
      self.current_user = find_current_user
    end

    def disconnect
    end

    protected
      def find_current_user
        if current_user = User.find_by(id: cookies.signed[:user_id])
          current_user
        else
          reject_unauthorized_connection
        end
      end
  end
end
```

As discussed earlier, as the WebSocket connection is initiated by a HTTP request, any relevant cookies are passed to us. With these, we can find the User model for the signed-in user. If no user is found, the connection is rejected.

The statement `identified_by :current_user` marks `current_user` as an identifier for this specific connection, and it is also available as a delegate for all channels created for this connection. This is necessary so that we can refer to the connection made to a user within the channel objects.

We should now enable Action Cable in the client-side JavaScript code. The Rails application generator created a file app/assets/javascripts/cable.coffee. If you take a look at this, you will see the Asset Pipeline directives to include the Action Cable library and to load and files within the `channels` directory, as shown in Listing 6-10.

Listing 6-10. The Generated cable.coffee File

```
# Action Cable provides the framework to deal with WebSockets in Rails.
# You can generate new channels where WebSocket features live using the
rails generate channel command.
#
#= require action_cable
#= require_self
#= require_tree ./channels

(function() {
  this.App || (this.App = {});

  App.cable = ActionCable.createConsumer();

}).call(this);
```

The ActionCable.createConsumer() command can take a parameter to specify the URL of the Action Cable server, however it is best to omit this parameter and configure the cable server URL in the Rails environment setting, as we will see later in this chapter.

Finally, to complete the setup we need to enable the Action Cable server to be accessed via the rails server. To do this, you need to add a configuration setting. Edit the config/application.rb file to include the mount_point configuration, as shown in Listing 6-11.

Listing 6-11. Specifying a Mount Point for the Action Cable Server

```
require_relative 'boot'

require 'rails/all'

# Require the gems listed in Gemfile, including any gems
# you've limited to :test, :development, or :production.
Bundler.require(*Rails.groups)

module Livechat
  class Application < Rails::Application
    # Settings in config/environments/* take precedence over those
    specified here.
    # Application configuration should go into files in config/initializers
    # -- all .rb files in that directory are automatically loaded.
    config.action_cable.mount_path = '/cable'

  end
end
```

Creating a Messaging Channel

Now that we have a connection configured, we can begin creating channels. Each Action Cable connection can subscribe to one or more Action Cable *channels*. Once subscribed to a channel, the browser code can listen and transmit messages back and forth to the server at will.

To enable real-time messaging, we will create a channel called messages. There is a Rails generator to create the stub files for us. Run this now.

```
$ rails generate channel Messages
```

```
      create   app/channels/messages_channel.rb

      create   app/assets/javascripts/channels/messages.coffee
```

Server-Side Code

First, let's write the server-side code for this channel. Open the generated messages_channel.rb file. You will see the generated class, as shown in Listing 6-12.

Listing 6-12. The generated Messages Channel file

```
# Be sure to restart your server when you modify this file. Action Cable
runs in a loop that does not support auto reloading.
class MessagesChannel < ApplicationCable::Channel
  def subscribed
    # stream_from "some_channel"
  end

  def unsubscribed
    # Any cleanup needed when channel is unsubscribed
  end
end
```

Unsurprisingly, the subscribed method is executed whenever a client subscribes to a channel. The most common action to be included here is to initiated streaming from a Pub/Sub queue to the client's subscribers. This is done using the stream_from command.

Change the subscribed method to the following:

```
def subscribed
  stream_from "messages"
end
```

This means than any messages that are broadcast via the Pub/Sub queue called messages will be directly relayed to any subscribing clients. In turn, the client will then process or display the broadcast message.

In this case, since we only have one message room, we only need a single channel called messages. If we were to have different messages boards, when the client subscribes to a channel, it would pass a parameter that we could use as part of the queue name, for example:

```
stream_from "messages_room_#{params[:id]}"
```

We currently don't need to perform any actions when a client unsubscribes from a channel, so we can leave the unsubscribe method empty.

We now need to write the code to actually specify the message to send via the channel and to initiate the broadcast. This is done using the command ActionCable. server.broadcast, specifying the channel name and the data to broadcast. Since we want to initiate the broadcast when a new message is create, we can do this in MessageController create method.

As for what data to send - we have two options here. Either we can send just the text of the chat message sent by the user or we can send an HTML fragment.

In the case of just sending the text of the message, the client code would then be responsible for how the message is presented on the page. The issue with this is that the HTML would then be duplicated in two places - the Rails partial view file _message.html.erb, and the JavaScript client-side code.

To solve this, we can use the existing HTML partial view file to create the HTML which in-turn is then broadcast to the clients, simplifying the client-side code and meaning that you only have to maintain one set of HTML templates.

Of course, which method you use depends entirely what your requirements are and you should use whichever makes the most sense for your application.

Go back to your messages_controller.rb file and modify the create method to broadcast the message partial view rather than performing a redirect, as shown in Listing 6-13.

Listing 6-13. Changes to the Messages Controller to support Action Cable

```
def create
  @message = current_user.messages.create! body: params[:message][:body]
  ActionCable.server.broadcast "messages", render(
    partial: 'messages/message',
    object: @message
  )
end
```

This conveniently makes use of the new Rails 5 feature that allows partials to be rendered from anywhere.

In a production application, you may prefer to perform this broadcast in an asynchronous job using Active Job.

Client -Side Code

We now need to write the client-side code for the live chat feature. But first, we need to make one small change to the new message form.

Open app/views/messages/index.html.erb and change the form_for statement to add remote: true, as shown in Listing 6-14.

Listing 6-14. Messages Index View changed to a remote form

```erb
<h2>Messages</h2>
<%= form_for :message, remote: true do |form| %>
  <%= form.text_field :body %>
  <%= form.submit 'Send Message' %>
<% end %>
```

This change means that the message create request is done as a JavaScript AJAX request, so the browser won't automatically reload the page after the form is submitted.

Now edit the generated messages channel CoffeeScript file, app/assets/ javascripts/channels/messages.coffee. As you can see, the default callbacks for connected, disconnected, and received are stubbed out for you. Since we simply want to append any message HTML partials that are received via the channel, simply add the jQuery statement as shown in Listing 6-15.

Listing 6-15. The client-side Messages Channel code

```coffee
App.messages = App.cable.subscriptions.create "MessagesChannel",
  connected: ->
        # Called when the subscription is ready for use on the server

  disconnected: ->
        # Called when the subscription has been terminated by the server

  received: (data) ->
        # Called when there's incoming data on the websocket for this
        # channel
        $('#messages').append(data)
```

Running the Application

Before trying out the application, you need to ensure that Redis is running. If you haven't already started it, you can start it up in a new terminal window using redis-server.

Since we have added the Action Cable mount to the routes.rb file, we only need to run a single Rails process, so start as usual:

```
$ rails s
```

As before, open two different browsers, for example Safari and Chrome. Go to http://localhost:3000 on each and login as different people.

Now, with both windows open side by side, enter a chat message into the form. The message will immediately appear in both windows.

If you look at the Rails server log, you will see the broadcast message being sent to all the subscribed browsers when a new message is created.

Running in Production

As previously mentioned, you have the option of running Action Cable as an in-app server or as a standalone process. When you go to run your Action Cable application in production you may wish to run the Action Cable server separate from your normal Rails app to allow you to scale them separately as necessary.

However, this obviously complicates the setup and configuration of your deployment. You may wish to start simple and switch when necessary.

We will briefly look at the configuration options available when setting up your application for something other than the default in-app development mode.

Action Cable URL

If you are running a standalone Action Cable server, you should set the URL where the Action Cable server can be accessed. This is likely to be a subdomain of your site, a different port on your main site or as a directory on your domain (such as /cable).

You should set this in your production.rb environment configuration file as config. action_cable.url. Simply pass in the URL of your Action Cable server as a string. If you are using SSL, you must use the prefix wss://, if not, ws://.

For example:

```
config.action_cable.url = 'wss://apress.com:2000/cable'
```

When you set this configuration variable, Rails uses it for the action_cable_meta_ tag, which is used in the layout app/views/layouts/application.html.erb. Adding the following helper to the header of your layout file allows you to customise the URL of you Action Cable server.

```
<%= action_cable_meta_tag %>
```

If you look in the source HTML of your development application, you see this expands to the following:

```
<meta name="action-cable-url" content="/cable" />
```

This obviously shows your production action_cable.url in production mode rather than the relative URL /cable.

Allowed Request Origins

Action Cable only accepts request from whitelisted domains, meaning that you must pass in the domain of your site as a configuration option.

You do this by setting `config.action_cable.allowed_request_origins` in your `production.rb` environment file. You pass in any domains that your application will be run on as an array. You can also use regular expressions in this array. For example:

```
config.action_cable.allowed_request_origins = [ 'http://apress.com',
/http:\/\/apress.*/ ]
```

Standalone Mode

The Action Cable server is just a Rack application, so if you add a simple Rack configuration file, you can start the Action Cable server using puma or thin.

For example, add the Rack config file `cable_config.ru`:

```
require ::File.expand_path('../config/environment', __FILE__)
Rails.application.eager_load!

run Action Cable.server
```

This can then be started using Puma as an application server:

```
bundle exec puma -p 3010 cable_config.ru
```

Then, by setting the `config.action_cable.url` configuration option as described, your application connects to this cable server.

In production, this would be made available through a web server such as NGINX, allowing you to load balance and route to multiple Action Cable servers if necessary.

Summary

As you can see, Action Cable opens up a whole new type of application to Rails developers. If used sensibly, it has the potential to greatly improve the interactivity of Rails applications and makes it possible to easily develop types of web applications that were very difficult to write using Rails before.

Index

Get the eBook for only $5!

Why limit yourself?

Now you can take the weightless companion with you wherever you go and access your content on your PC, phone, tablet, or reader.

Since you've purchased this print book, we're happy to offer you the eBook in all 3 formats for just $5.

Convenient and fully searchable, the PDF version enables you to easily find and copy code—or perform examples by quickly toggling between instructions and applications. The MOBI format is ideal for your Kindle, while the ePUB can be utilized on a variety of mobile devices.

To learn more, go to www.apress.com/companion or contact support@apress.com.

Printed in the United States
By Bookmasters